1

College Oral Communication

HOUGHTON MIFFLIN
ENGLISH FOR ACADEMIC SUCCESS

Marsha J. Chan
Mission College

SERIES EDITORS

Patricia Byrd

Joy M. Reid

Cynthia M. Schuemann

Houghton Mifflin Company
Boston   New York

Publisher: Patricia A. Coryell
Director of ESL Publishing: Susan Maguire
Senior Development Editor: Kathy Sands Boehmer
Editorial Assistant: Evangeline Bermas
Senior Project Editor: Kathryn Dinovo
Manufacturing Assistant: Karmen Chong
Senior Marketing Manager: Annamarie Rice
Marketing Assistant: Andrew Whitacre

Cover graphics: LMA Communications, Natick, Massachusetts

Photo credits: © Gunter Marx/Corbis, top, p. 2; © Ariel Skelley/Corbis, bottom, p. 2; © Robert Dowling/Corbis, bottom, p. 3; © Japak Photo Library/Corbis, p. 38; © Becky Luigart-Stayner/Corbis, top left, p. 39; © Royalty-Free/Corbis, top right, p. 39; © Lois Ellen Frank/Corbis, bottom left, p. 39; © David Thomas/Corbis, bottom right, p. 39; © Charles Rotkin/Corbis, p. 89; © Steve Raymer/Corbis, p. 123; © Royalty-Free/Corbis, p. 139; © John Henley/Corbis, p. 167; © Bettmann/Corbis, p. 174; © Hulton-Deutsch Collections/Corbis, left, p. 196; © Bettmann/Corbis, right, p. 196; © Bettmann/Corbis, p. 197; © Helen King/Corbis, top, p. 208; © Jim Craigmyle/Corbis, bottom, p. 208; © Royalty-Free/Corbis, p. 209; © Richard Hutchings/Corbis, p. 209; © Tom & Dee Ann McCarthy/Corbis, p. 209; © Ed Bock/Corbis, p. 209; and two screenshots from Google. Copyright © Google, Inc. Reprinted with permission, p. 247

Text credits: Better Sleep Council's survey. Reprinted with permission of the Better Sleep Council. www.bettersleep.org, p. 131; "How Sleepy Are You" From THE EPWORTH SLEEPINESS SCALE. Reprinted by permission of Dr. Murray W. Johns, p. 161

Printed in the U.S.A.

Library of Congress Control Number: 2004112192

ISBN: 0-618-23016-5

3456789-CRW-08 07

Contents

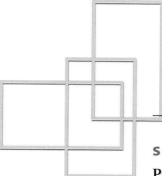

Houghton Mifflin English for Academic Success Series

SERIES EDITORS

Patricia Byrd, Joy M. Reid, Cynthia M. Schuemann

What Is the Purpose of This Series?

The Houghton Mifflin English for Academic Success series is a comprehensive program of student and instructor materials: four levels of student language proficiency textbooks in three skill areas (oral communication, reading, and writing), with supplemental vocabulary textbooks at each level. For instructors and students, a useful website supports classroom teaching, learning, and assessment. For instructors, four Essentials of Teaching Academic Language books (*Essentials of Teaching Academic Oral Communication, Essentials of Teaching Academic Reading, Essentials of Teaching Academic Writing,* and *Essentials of Teaching Academic Vocabulary*) provide helpful information for instructors new to teaching oral communication, reading, writing, and vocabulary.

The fundamental purpose of the series is to prepare students who are not native speakers of English for academic success in U.S. college degree programs. By studying these materials, students in college English for Academic Purposes (EAP) courses will gain the academic language skills they need to be successful students in degree programs. Additionally, students will learn about being successful students in U.S. college courses.

The series is based on considerable prior research as well as our own investigations of students' needs and interests, instructors' needs and desires, and institutional expectations and requirements. For example, our survey research revealed what problems instructors feel they face in their classrooms and what they actually teach; who the students are and what they know and do not know about the "culture" of U.S. colleges; and what types of exams are required for admission at various colleges.

Student Audience

The materials in this series are for college-bound ESL students at U.S. community colleges and undergraduate programs at other institutions. Some of these students are U.S. high school graduates. Some of them are long-term U.S. residents who graduated from a high school before coming to the United States. Others are newer U.S. residents. Still others are more typical international students. All of them need to develop academic language skills and knowledge of ways to be successful in U.S. college degree courses.

All of the books in this series have been created to implement the Houghton Mifflin English for Academic Success competencies. These competencies are based on those developed by ESL instructors and administrators in Florida, California, and Connecticut to be the underlying structure for EAP courses at colleges in those states. These widely respected competencies assure that the materials meet the real world needs of EAP students and instructors.

All of the books focus on . . .

- Starting where the students are, building on their strengths and prior knowledge (which is considerable, if not always academically relevant), and helping students self-identify needs and plans to strengthen academic language skills
- Academic English, including development of Academic Vocabulary and grammar required by students for academic speaking/listening, reading, and writing
- Master Student Skills, including learning style analysis, strategy training, and learning about the "culture" of U.S. colleges, which lead to their becoming successful students in degree courses and degree programs
- Topics and readings that represent a variety of academic disciplinary areas so that students learn about the language and content of the social sciences, the hard sciences, education, and business as well as the humanities

All of the books provide…

- Interesting and valuable content that helps the students develop their knowledge of academic content as well as their language skills and student skills
- A wide variety of practical classroom-tested activities that are easy to teach and engage the students

- Assessment tools at the end of each chapter so that instructors have easy-to-implement ways to assess student learning and students have opportunities to assess their own growth
- Websites for the students and for the instructors: the student sites will provide additional opportunities to practice reading, writing, listening, vocabulary development, and grammar. The instructor sites will provide instructor's manuals, teaching notes and answer keys, value-added materials like handouts and overheads that can be reproduced to use in class, and assessment tools such as additional tests to use beyond the assessment materials in each book.

▭ What Is the Purpose of the Oral Communication Strand?

The Oral Communication strand of Houghton Mifflin English for Academic Success focuses on development of speaking and listening skills necessary for college study. Dedicated to meeting academic needs of students by teaching them how to handle the spoken English used by instructors and students in college classrooms, the four books provide engaging activities to practice both academic listening and academic speaking. Students learn to participate effectively in a variety of academic situations, including discussions, lectures, student study groups, and office meetings with their college instructors.

Because of the importance of academic vocabulary in the spoken English of the classroom, the oral communication strand teaches the students techniques for learning and using new academic vocabulary both to recognize the words when they hear them and to use the words in their own spoken English. Grammar appropriate to the listening and speaking activities is also included in each chapter. For example, Book 2 includes work with the pronunciation of irregular past tense verbs as part of learning how to listen to and participate in academic discussions focused on history. In addition to language development, the books provide for academic skill development through the teaching of appropriate academic tasks and the giving of master student tips to help students better understand what is expected of them in college classes. Students learn to carry out academic tasks in ways that are linguistically, academically, and culturally appropriate. For example, students learn how to take information from the spoken presentations by their instructors and then to use that information for other academic tasks such as tests or small group discussions. That is, students are not taught to take notes for some abstract reason but learn to make a powerful connection between note-taking and success in other assigned tasks.

Each book has a broad disciplinary theme to give coherence to the content. These themes were selected because of their high interest for students; they are also topics commonly explored in introductory college courses and so provide useful background for students. Materials were selected that are academically appropriate but that do not require expert knowledge by the instructor. The following themes are used: Book 1: People and Human Behavior, Book 2: The Connections between Human Beings and Animals, Book 3: Communication and Media, and Book 4: Money. For example, Book 1 has one chapter about the psychological effects of music and another on the relationship between laughter and people's social, psychological, and medical well-being. Book 2 uses topics such as taboo foods, animals as workers, using animals in medical and scientific testing, along with one of Aesop's fables. Book 3 includes the history of movies, computer animation, privacy rights, and other topics related to modern media. Book 4 takes on a topic that fascinates most students with various themes related to money, including such related topics as the history of money, marketing use of psychological conditioning, and the economics of the World Wide Web. These topics provide high-interest content for use in the listening and speaking activities, but do not require that instructors have to develop any new knowledge to be able to use the materials.

Instructor Support Materials

Recorded materials presented in each chapter are available on an audiotape or CD that is provided with each book. In addition to a recording of the main lecture for each chapter, the recording includes other materials such as dialogues and academic vocabulary.

The series also includes a resource book for instructors called *Essentials of Teaching Academic Oral Communication* by John Murphy. This practical book provides strategies and activities for the use of instructors new to the teaching of oral communication.

⬚ What Is the Organization of *College Oral Communication 1*?

College Oral Communication 1 prepares low-intermediate level students for the demands of college-level academic listening and speaking tasks. Six chapters of lectures and dialogues about music appreciation, nutrition, geography, human biology and psychology as related to sleep debt, psychology, sociology, and medicine as related to laughter, and general business and technology present concepts and language that many students will encounter in future college courses.

Vocabulary is a prominent feature of the textbook. Each chapter provides a list of academic words related to the lecture and dialogues supported by pronunciation work in syllable number and stress.

Master Student Tips scattered throughout the textbook provide students with short comments on a particular strategy, activity, or practical advice to follow in an academic setting.

Chapter Organization

Each chapter is clearly divided into three sections: Effective Academic Listening, Effective Academic Speaking, and Assessing Your Academic Listening and Speaking Skills.

Effective Academic Listening

Getting Ready for the Lecture Warm-up discussion questions, illustrations, charts, and tables engage students in the content and prepare them to listen and take notes from the lecture.

Looking at Language Identifying syllables and stress in words, taking dictation, using a dictionary, pronouncing academic vocabulary, listening to the vocabulary of academic lectures in context, and learning language patterns used frequently in the lecture are featured in this part.

Getting Information from the Lecture Students practice a variety of listening strategies and are guided toward successful comprehension of the lecture by predicting content; understanding organization; listening for key words, numbers, and discourse markers; recognizing main ideas and details, and taking brief notes with an outline or in answer to questions.

Using Your Notes Students participate in academic tasks directly related to their notes and the content of the particular chapter, such as discussing notes in study groups, answering test questions, and applying information from the lecture to a case study.

Effective Academic Speaking

Activities in this section develop ESL learners' skills in speaking to further their success in the types of oral communication tasks expected of students in a college environment. These listening and speaking tasks include retelling the content of the lecture, participating in small group discussions on the lecture theme, presenting short talks on related topics and taking notes, and talking about personal experiences related to the chapter content. Also included in this section are dialogues for practicing the pronunciation, stress, intonation, vocabulary and grammar of questions and answers; information gaps with language patterns and charts or maps as springboards for communication; and other expansion activities, such as performing a simple dance that relates the rhythm of music to the rhythm of language. Self-check activities encourage students to reflect upon their learning and attainment of the objectives.

Assessing Your Listening and Speaking Skills

As they review the chapter content, students apply information and skills in writing, listening, and speaking to demonstrate that they have mastered the objectives of the chapter. They orally review vocabulary and sentence patterns for pronunciation, stress, and fluency. They take dictation of academic vocabulary and concepts related to the chapter theme. Each chapter ends with a listing of the chapter objectives and a self-assessment tool for students to evaluate their progress. Tests and quizzes may be downloaded by instructors from the Houghton Mifflin website.

Acknowledgments

This book and its accompanying media are the result of the dedication, determination, industriousness, and collaboration of many people. The Houghton Mifflin Senior Development Editor, Kathy Sands Boehmer, under the direction of Susan Maguire, Director of ESL Publishing, skillfully presented *College Oral Communication 1* in its proper light within the expansive English for Academic Success series.

Mentor and editor of the Oral Communication strand, H. Patricia Byrd, with gifted grace and talent, kept us authors on the path to creation and completion and provided invaluable insights. Together with her series co-editors, Joy M. Reid and Cynthia Schuemann, the editorial team provided outstanding structure and guidance.

I am indebted to my ESL colleagues at Mission College, Marianne Brems, Joan Powers, Kara Dworak, Cheryl Hertig, and Julaine Rosner, faithful advisors who painstakingly reviewed manuscripts, field-tested the materials with students, and provided indispensable suggestions. Their contributions to the content, form, and function of the book are indelible. My fellow College Oral Communication authors, Ann E. Roemer, Cheryl L. Delk, and Steve Jones, were also available on a regular basis for consultation, development, advice, and laughter that provided motivation and support for the project.

I extend my sincere appreciation to the excellent comments and constructive criticism offered on the manuscript by reviewers from colleges across the nation:

Richard Cervin, Sacramento City College
Miranda Joyce Childe, Miami Dade Community College
Kristina de los Santos, Baltimore City Community College
Tatiana Erohina, Santa Ana College and Irvine Valley College
Laura Horani, Portland Community College
Lisa Kader, Massasoit Community College
John Kostovich, Miami-Dade Community College
Maria Schimke, Green River Community College
Shirley Terrell, Collin County Community College
Mark Tremper, Glendale Community College
Krista Valenzuela-Emanuel, Chandler-Gilbert Community College
Hoda Zaki, Camden County College
Kathy Zuo, William Rainey Harper College

For their time and talent recording the pilot versions of my sound tracks, I am extremely grateful to Peter Anning, Scott Brunson, Scott Chan, Frank Chong, Charlie Cutten, Rob Dewis, Kara Dworak, Joseph Ordaz, Jane Patton, Julaine Rosner, Stefan Rosner, Heather Lynne Rothenburg, and Terry Yang.

The hundreds of students who field-tested the materials deserve special mention. Their willingness to try out new methods and materials and their resulting responses and suggestions led to the improvement of the text. Their dedication to learning reinforced my commitment to providing them the means to meet their linguistic and academic goals.

Finally, I thank my family and friends for their unwavering love, encouragement, and support in this multi-faceted project.

▭ What Student Competencies Are Covered in *College Oral Communication 1*?

Houghton Mifflin English for Academic Success Competencies
College Oral Communication 1

Description of Overall Purposes

Students develop listening and speaking skills necessary for participating in classroom discussions with an emphasis on clarification through rewording and asking questions.

With the Materials in This Book, a Student Will Learn:

Production

Competency 1: The student will participate in classroom discussions with emphasis on narrating and describing situations to develop oral communication skills including fluency, idea sequencing, accuracy, vocabulary, and pronunciation.

Competency 2: The student will demonstrate the ability to ask and answer questions, reword statements, and ask for clarification.

Competency 3: The student will actively participate and be sufficiently understood in role-playing, simulating simple academic situations.

Competency 4: The student will learn about and develop level appropriate strategies for helping others to understand her/him.

Comprehension

Competency 5: The student will understand questions and directions appropriate to the level.

Competency 6: The student will understand the main idea and major and minor details of a short lecture.

Competency 7: The student will be able to draw conclusions, make simple predictions, and relate the content of a short lecture to personal experience.

Competency 8: The student will take simple dictation of connected discourse as the basis for developing skill at note-taking during lectures and discussions.

▭ What Are the Features of the Oral Communication Books?

The Houghton Mifflin English for Academic Success series is a comprehensive program of student and instructor materials. The fundamental purpose of the program is to prepare students who are not native speakers of English for academic success in U.S. college degree programs.

The Oral Communication strand of the Houghton Mifflin English for Academic Success series focuses on development of speaking and listening skills necessary for college study. Dedicated to meeting academic needs of students by teaching them how to handle the spoken English used by instructors and students in college classrooms, the four books provide engaging activities to practice both academic listening and academic speaking. Students learn to participate effectively in a variety of academic situations, including discussions, lectures, study groups, and office meetings with their college instructors.

Broad Disciplinary Themes: Each book has a broad disciplinary theme to give coherence to the content. These themes were selected because of their high interest for students. They are also topics commonly explored in introductory college courses and so provide useful background for students.

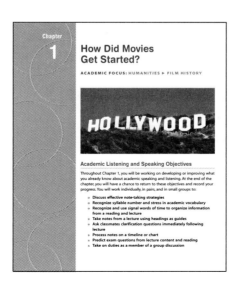

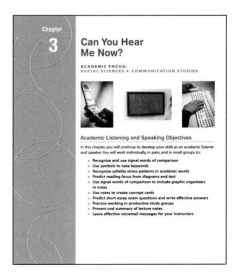

Effective Academic Listening: Students listen to authentic classroom interactions and lectures. They learn to take information from the spoken presentations and use their notes for other academic tasks such as tests or small group discussions.

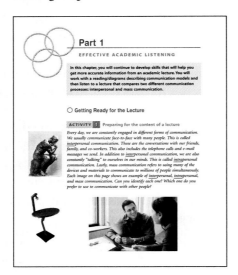

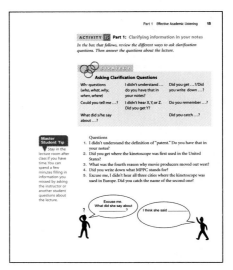

Effective Academic Speaking: Speaking tasks resemble types of academic tasks expected of students in the college environment. These speaking tasks include taking on roles and participating in small group formal and informal discussions on lecture content, presenting oral summaries, to leaving effective voicemail messages. Students learn to do oral presentations appropriate to their proficiency level and to college study.

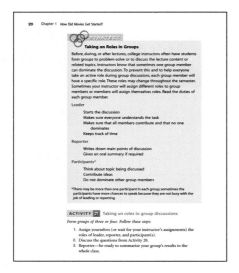

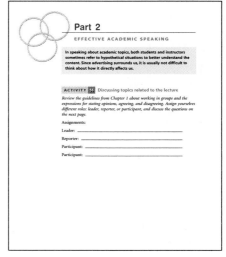

Self-Assessment of Academic Listening and Speaking Skills: Students are given the opportunity to reflect on several of the academic strategies they learned and practiced in the chapters. Each chapter ends with a listing of the chapter objectives for students to evaluate their progress.

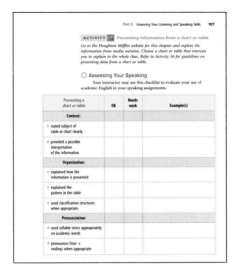

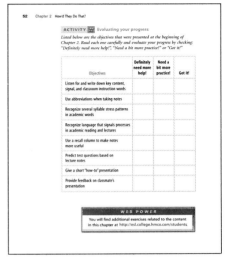

Academic Vocabulary: The Oral Communication strand teaches students techniques for learning and using new academic vocabulary in order to recognize the words when they hear them and to also use the words in their own spoken English.

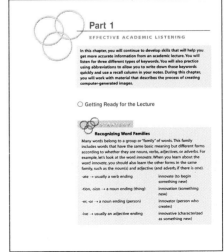

Academic Listening and Speaking Strategies: Key strategies and skills are interspersed throughout each book. Students can clearly see important concepts to focus on as they complete the activities in each chapter. Highlighted strategies will help students improve both their listening and speaking skills.

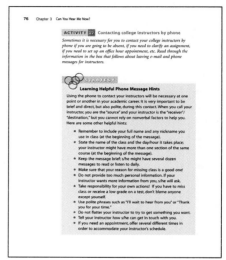

Master Student Tips: Master Student Tips throughout the textbooks provide students with short comments on a particular strategy, activity, or practical advice to follow in an academic setting. Instructors can use these tips to help students become better students by building their understanding of college study.

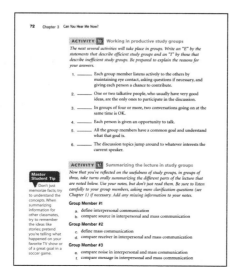

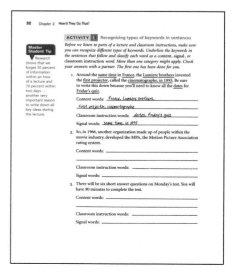

Power Grammar Boxes: Students can be very diverse in their grammar and rhetorical needs so each chapter contains Power Grammar boxes that introduce the grammar structures students need to be fluent and accurate in academic English.

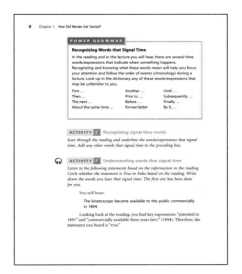

Ancillary Program: The following items are available to accompany the Houghton Mifflin English for Academic Success series Oral Communication strand.

- Instructor website: Additional teaching materials, activities, and robust student assessment.
- Student website: Additional exercises and activities.
- Audio Program: Available on either CD-ROM or cassette.
- The Houghton Mifflin English for Academic Success series Vocabulary books: You can choose the appropriate level to shrinkwrap with your text.
- *Essentials of Teaching Academic Oral Communication* by John Murphy is available for purchase. It gives you theoretical and practical information for teaching oral communication.

1

The Power of Music

ACADEMIC FOCUS: HUMANITIES ▶ MUSIC

Academic Listening and Speaking Objectives

In this chapter, you will develop your skills as an academic listener and speaker. You will hear a short lecture about ways that music has power over its listeners. Also, you will learn to pronounce academic vocabulary, and you will practice discussing academic topics. You will participate in listening, speaking, moving, and thinking activities. In particular, you will:

- Develop vocabulary and expressions to discuss music
- Use a dictionary to learn the pronunciation of new academic words
- Hear, identify, and pronounce key vocabulary with proper syllables and word stress
- Hear and pronounce present tense endings /s/, /z/, and /ɪz/
- Complete an outline with details
- Use *make* in causative sentences
- Ask questions for clarification and repetition
- Retell the main points of the lecture
- Use falling intonation on statements and Wh- questions
- Use rising intonation on Yes-No questions
- Ask and answer questions about likes and dislikes
- Take dictation of sentences related to music

Part 1

In a Music Appreciation course, you listen to different kinds of music. Some of the things you learn about are rhythm,[1] harmony,[2] and form. Learning about these elements helps you develop a greater understanding and a deeper appreciation of all styles of music.

Getting Ready for the Lecture

ACTIVITY 1 Discussing music and movement

In a small group of three or four students, look at the illustrations. Discuss the questions with your partners and make notes. Describe the person or people in the pictures. Where are they? What kinds of music or musical instrument are they playing? What kinds of movements are they making? Put a check (✓) by the scenes that you think are interesting. Share your observations with your classmates.

A.	
	Person
	Place
	Music or instrument
	Movement

B.	
	People
	Place
	Music or instrument
	Movement

1. *rhythm* (*n.*) = regular beat, especially in music or movement
2. *harmony* (*n.*) = a pleasing combination of musical sounds; the study of the way musical chords are constructed and work in relation to one another

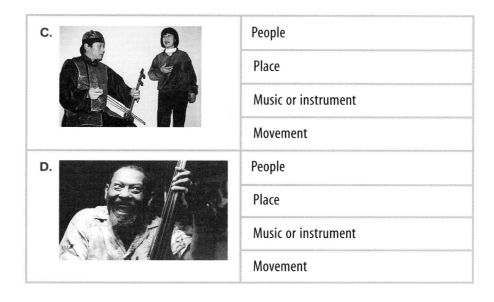

C.	People
	Place
	Music or instrument
	Movement
D.	People
	Place
	Music or instrument
	Movement

Music Appreciation Classes

In a music appreciation class, students listen to different kinds, or genres,[3] of music. They learn to identify and appreciate them. Your instructor may present examples of music in class or may ask you to study examples in the library or on the Web.

ACTIVITY 2 Listening to different kinds of music

Discuss the following genres of music with your class. Do you know the names of artists or songs? What other genres of music are you familiar with?

Classical	Country	Rock	Jazz

3. *genre* (*n.*) = a specific type of literature, art, or music grouped according to a style or subject: *classical, jazz*

▭ **Looking at Language**

> **Syllables**
>
> In speech, words are spoken with *syllables*. Clap twice, and you make the sound of two syllables. Many English words have more than one syllable. For example, *music* has two syllables: mu-sic.

 ACTIVITY 3 **Studying syllables**

Listen to the syllables in these words. Circle the number of syllables in each word. The first one is done for you

connection 1 2 ③ 4   instrument 1 2 3 4   anxiety   1 2 3 4

calm   1 2 3 4   academic   1 2 3 4   excited   1 2 3 4

relaxed   1 2 3 4   rhythm   1 2 3 4   pronounce 1 2 3 4

Listen again. Clap or tap the number of syllables you hear.

Pronounce each word with the correct number of syllables. Clap as you speak.

 **STRATEGY**

Marking Syllables and Stress

When a word has two or more syllables, one syllable is stressed. A stressed syllable is longer and stronger than an unstressed syllable. For example, *mu-sic* has two syllables. *Mu-sic* is stressed on the first syllable.

Syllable-Stress Code

We can write this information with a pair of numbers. We write the number of syllables before the dash and the stressed syllable after the dash. This is the *syllable-stress code*.

mu-sic [2 – 1]

This word has two syllables. It is stressed on the first syllable.

ACTIVITY 4   **Identifying syllables and word stress**

Listen to these words. Write the syllable-stress code to indicate the number of syllables and the stressed syllable. The first one is done for you. The word emotion *has three syllables and is stressed on the second syllable.*

1. e•mo•tion   [_3_ - _2_]   5. straight   [___ - ___]

2. en•ter•tain   [___ - ___]   6. prob•a•bly   [___ - ___]

3. nerv•ous•ness [___ - ___]   7. in•stru•ment [___ - ___]

4. dic•tion•ar•y [___ - ___]   8. rhy•thm   [___ - ___]

Pronounce the words after your instructor. Hear and feel the number of syllables and the stressed syllable in each word.

 ACTIVITY 5   **Taking dictation**

Master Student Tip

▼ Listen to syllables and word stress. This can make it easy for you to understand new words when you hear them. Practice syllables and stress. This will make it easier for you to pronounce words clearly. Listen and feel the beat and rhythm of words.

Learning to take dictation is an important skill. Taking dictation builds and assesses many language skills. Dictation can help you sharpen your listening skill, grammar ability, reading comprehension, and vocabulary knowledge.

You will hear the words from Activity 4 in sentences. You will hear each sentence three times. First, listen and try to understand the meaning of the whole sentence. Second, listen and write. Third, listen and check. Use the number of words in the parentheses as a guide.

1. _____ (7 words)

2. _____ (6 words)

3. _____ (8 words)

4. _____ (8 words)

5. _____ (5 words)

6. _____ (8 words)

7. _____ (6 words)

8. _____ (10 words)

ACTIVITY 6 **Using a dictionary to find syllables and stress**

A dictionary is a very useful resource. It contains an alphabetical list of words, with information given for each word, called the *entry word*. The information usually includes pronunciation, definitions, and word origin.

Many American English dictionaries show each entry word with a dot • between syllables. This word division is called *syllabification*.[4]

The American Heritage Dictionary shows the pronunciation of a word in parentheses, with a heavy mark ´ after the stressed syllable.

musician   mu•si•cian   (myo͞o-zĭsh´ ən)

The word *musician* has three syllables and is stressed on the second syllable. The syllable-stress code is [3-2]. Look at the pronunciation key in the dictionary to learn what sound each symbol means. Other dictionaries use different symbols. Study how syllables and stress are shown in your dictionary.

Look up the following words in your English dictionary. After each entry word, copy the pronunciation information. Then write the syllable-stress code.

Name of dictionary: _____

1. sentence   _____ _____   [__ - __]

2. pronounce _____ _____   [__ - __]

3. definition _____ _____   [__ - __]

Answer the questions.

1. Does your dictionary indicate syllables (word division)? ____ If so, how? _____

2. Does your dictionary indicate stress? ____ If so, how?

_____

4. Written and spoken syllabification are not always the same. Compare.
   Same   written and spoken: mu•si•cian
   Different   written: nerv•ous•ness   spoken: ner•vous•ness

ACTIVITY 7   Learning the vocabulary of academic lectures

> **Academic Word List**
>
> The words in this section appear on the Academic Word List (AWL).*
> You will meet these words in many academic classes. If you learn these
> words well, it will help you in your coursework.
>
> *Coxhead, Averil (1998). *An Academic Word List.* Victoria University of Wellington,
> New Zealand. Go to the website for this book to learn more about the AWL.

*Look up these words in an English dictionary. Some words may be used
as both a verb and a noun, and others as both a noun and an adjective.
Look up the pronunciation of the part of speech⁵ given in parentheses.
Copy the syllabification and pronunciation of each word exactly. Write the
syllable-stress code. Study the definition. If the dictionary provides example
sentences, see how the word is used in context. Then compare your answers
with a classmate's. The first one is done for you.*

1. access   <u>ac•cess</u>   <u>(ăk´ sĕs)</u>   [<u>2</u> - <u>1</u>]
    (*tr.v.*)
    To obtain or retrieve from a storage device; as of
    information on a computer.

2. alter   _____   _____   [___ - ___]
    (*tr.v.*)
    To change or make different; modify.

3. chapter   _____   _____   [___ - ___]
    (*n.*)
    One of the main divisions of a long piece of
    writing, such as a book, that is usually numbered
    or titled.

4. classical   _____   _____   [___ - ___]
    (*n.*)
    (Music) Of or relating to music in the educated
    European tradition, such as symphony and opera,
    as opposed to popular or folk music.

5. concept   _____   _____   [___ - ___]
    (*n.*)
    A general idea, thought.

5. *part of speech* (*n. phr.*) = the function of a word, such as noun, verb, adjective, or
   adverb

6. culture
   (*n.*)
   _____   _____   [__ - __]

   The ideas, activities (art, foods, businesses), and ways of behaving that are special to a country, people, or region.

7. expand
   (*intr.v.*)
   _____   _____   [__ - __]

   To grow larger in size, volume, or quantity.

8. file
   (*n.*)
   _____   _____   [__ - __]

   A folder, box, space on a computer disk, etc. used for holding information.

9. focus
   (*tr.v.*)
   _____   _____   [__ - __]

   To center one's attention on sthg. (sthg = something)

10. identify
   (*tr.v.*)
   _____   _____   [__ - __]

   To recognize who sbdy is or what sthg is. (sbdy = somebody)

11. individual
   (*n.*)
   _____   _____   [__ - __]

   Single, separate.

12. injure
   (*tr.v.*)
   _____   _____   [__ - __]

   To hurt, cause damage.

13. job
   (*n.*)
   _____   _____   [__ - __]

   Work that one is paid to do every day; a specific task, piece of work.

14. lecture
   (*n.*)
   _____   _____   [__ - __]

   A speech on a topic.

15. major
   (*n.*)
   _____   _____   [__ - __]

   Main, most important.

16. minor
   (*n.*)
   _____   _____   [__ - __]

   Lesser in importance or smaller in amount or size.

17. physical
   (*n.*)
   _____   _____   [__ - __]

   Of or related to the body.

18. react
   (*tr.v.*)

_____   _____   [__ - __]

To speak or move when sthg happens.

19. relax
   (*intr.v.*)

_____   _____   [__ - __]

To stop being nervous, angry, or busy and enjoy oneself.

20. stress
   (*n.*)

_____   _____   [__ - __]

Mental or physical strain or difficulty caused by pressure.

21. tense
   (*adj.*)

_____   _____   [__ - __]

Nervous, tight and stiff; anxious.

ACTIVITY 8   Checking and pronouncing academic words

Listen to the pronunciation of each word in the previous activity. Check the syllable-stress code.

Pronounce each word with your instructor or the recording, and then practice with a partner.

ACTIVITY 9   Listening to the academic words in context

Listen to the sentences and complete each one with a word from the academic word list in Activity 7. Sometimes you will hear different forms of the words on the list. Write the form that you hear.

1. If you have your student ID, you can _____ the files in the computer lab.

2. Music can make people want to move _____.

3. Right now, I'm _____ my attention on vocabulary.

4. Each singer has her or his _____ performance style.

5. My brother prefers rock music; I prefer _____.

6. When the baby's mother sang him a lullaby, he _____ by calming down and falling asleep.

7. The _____ soldiers were treated near the battlefield.

8. He gets very _____ and nervous before an exam.

9. She is full of _____ because her parents are seriously ill.

10. She takes a warm bath to _____ from her tension and worry.

11. The professor introduced the topic of musical notes on Monday and then _____ on it on Wednesday.

12. Food, art, businesses, ideas, and behaviors help define the _____ of a country or region.

13. Freedom of speech and the right to vote are two of the many _____ of democracy.

14. When he played a famous singer's song, he _____ the rhythm a bit.

15. I can _____ that song as country western.

16. Keep all of your _____ in this folder.

17. She fell on the _____ and got _____.

18. We'll listen to the _____ and listen for _____ and _____ details.

19. In this _____ of the book, we are learning about music.

POWER GRAMMAR

Verbs That End in -s or -es

The present tense is used to describe conditions and actions that usually happen or are true in general. In the lecture, you will hear many instances of the present tense. For third person singular (he, she, it), the verb ends in **-s** or **-es**. For example,

> Music <u>makes</u> people happy.
> Music <u>entertains</u> listeners.
> Music <u>relaxes</u> us.

ACTIVITY 10 **Listening to present tense endings**

In spoken English, the **-s** or **-es** endings are pronounced in three different ways: /s/, /z/, and /ɪz/. You can hear those ways in the pronunciation of <u>makes</u>, <u>entertains</u>, and <u>relaxes</u>.

Listen to the base form and the -s/-es forms of the following verbs.

Base form	Voiceless /s/	Base form	Voiced /z/	Base form	Extra syllable /ɪz/
get	gets	go	goes	focus	focuses
put	puts	play	plays	replace	replaces
lift	lifts	renew	renews	increase	increases
connect	connects	cheer	cheers	relax	relaxes
make	makes	stir	stirs	cause	causes
react	reacts	require	requires	wash	washes
take	takes	mean	means	push	pushes
help	helps	happen	happens	watch	watches
keep	keeps	entertain	entertains	research	researches
		bring	brings		
		control	controls		
		need	needs		
		nod	nods		
		build	builds		
		move	moves		

Pronounce each pair of words after your instructor or with the recording. Practice pronouncing the verbs with a partner.

ACTIVITY 11 Listening to verbs with and without -*s*/-*es*

Listen to the verb phrases. Underline the verb form you hear. The first one is done for you.

1. _____ (make / <u>makes</u>) people want to move their bodies.

2. _____ (react / reacts) in a physical way.

3. _____ (watch / watches) music shows.

4. _____ (help / helps) us hear clearly.

5. _____ (cheer / cheers) the performers.

6. _____ (focus / focuses) on -*s* endings.

7. _____ (bring / brings) people together.

8. _____ (entertain / entertains) listeners.

9. _____ (require / requires) careful listening.

10. _____ (increase / increases) your speaking ability.

Singular subjects take verbs with -s/-es endings. Plural subjects take verbs without -s/-es endings. Look at the subjects below. Choose a subject from the list and write it in the blank for each sentence above.

1. **a.** A strong rhythm   **b.** Beautiful songs

2. **a.** Your body   **b.** People

3. **a.** Tiffany   **b.** Tiffany and Bryan

4. **a.** A quiet room   **b.** Earphones

5. **a.** The audience   **b.** The listeners

6. **a.** This activity   **b.** These sentences

7. **a.** Good music   **b.** Fun parties

8. **a.** A talented musician   **b.** Performing artists

9. **a.** Good pronunciation   **b.** Good speaking skills

10. **a.** Constant practice   **b.** Time and effort

Complete the first sentence as follows:

1. <u>A strong rhythm</u> (make / <u>makes</u>) people want to move

   their bodies.

Work with a partner. Student A, choose a subject. Student B, repeat the subject and complete the sentence with the correct verb. Pay attention to /s/, /z/, and /ɪz/ endings. Take turns.

Examples:

Student A: Beautiful songs
Student B: Beautiful songs make people want to move
their bodies.

Student B: A strong rhythm
Student A: A strong rhythm makes people want to move
their bodies.

POWER GRAMMAR

Causative Sentences with *Make*

We often use the verb *make* to show cause and effect. Here are two common patterns you will hear in the lecture:

Pattern A. Make = to cause something to happen, to cause somebody to do something

Subject	+	*make*	+	object (sbdy/sthg)	+	base form verb
Music		makes		people		move.

Pattern B. *Make* = to cause a feeling or condition

Subject	+	*make*	+	object (sbdy/sthg)	+	adjective
Music		makes		people		happy.

ACTIVITY 12   Using *make* in causative sentences

Draw a box around the verb **make**, *circle the* **object**, *and underline* **the base form verb**. *The first one is done as a model. This is sentence pattern A.*

1. Music makes (people) want to move.

2. Listening to soft piano music makes me relax.

3. Do sad movies make you cry?

4. Those pictures on the wall make your house look beautiful.

Draw a box around the verb **make**, *circle the* **object**, *and draw a wavy line under the* **adjective**. *The first one is done as a model. This is sentence pattern B.*

1. Music makes (people) happy.

2. Eating peanuts makes him sick.

3. Does studying make us smart?

4. Tests don't make her nervous.

Complete the sentences with the correct form of the verb **make**. *Circle sentence pattern A or B.*

1. I like rock music. It _____ me dance!   A   B

2. Kevin likes to read. Reading _____ him happy.   A   B

3. Doing exercise regularly can _____ you strong and healthy.   A   B

4. Thanks for the flowers! They _____ the room cheerful.   A   B

5. That joke is really funny. It _____ everyone laugh.   A   B

6. She takes the medicine. It _____ her headache disappear.   A   B

▭ Getting Information from the Lecture

> Students listen to lectures to get information to use for tests and
> other assignments. The activities in this section help you learn to be
> an academic listener. First, you will listen to get information. Later, you
> will use that information to answer questions.
>   This short lecture is about the power of music to move people.

 ACTIVITY 13   Taking lecture notes about main ideas

At the beginning of the lecture, the instructor reminds students how
to access the files of different music genres in the music lab. He answers a
question about quizzes. This kind of information about how students have
to do assignments is often called *teacher talk*. Then he presents a new
topic. He describes six powers of music.

*Listen to the lecture. The formal part starts after one minute of teacher talk.
As you listen, try to find the answers to the following general question. Jot
down⁶ notes as you listen. You may listen more than once. Later, you will
use your notes to help you recall the information from the lecture.*

In what ways does music have the power to move people?

1. _____

2. _____

3. _____

4. _____

5. _____

6. _____

How many times did you need to listen to the lecture to jot down
the six powers of music?

   a. 1
   b. 2
   c. 3
   d. 4 or more

6. *jot down (v.phr.)* = to write down quickly for later reference

ACTIVITY 14 **Comprehending the lecture**

Listen to eight statements. Refer to your notes in Activity 13 and your auditory memory.[7] After listening to each statement, circle True or False according to your information.

1. True / False
2. True / False
3. True / False
4. True / False

5. True / False
6. True / False
7. True / False
8. True / False

STRATEGY

Understanding Outlines

Instructors often use an outline to prepare a lecture. In a well-organized lecture, the information usually focuses on one particular topic, or *theme*. It has major points and minor points.

A traditional outline form uses a series of numbers and letters to organize information. Roman numerals (I, II, III, etc.) are used to indicate major points. An indented series of letters (A, B, C, etc.) is used to indicate supporting information—a detail or example. Sometimes the lecture's theme appears in a statement before the first Roman numeral.

ACTIVITY 15 **Understanding outline form**

Look at the outline model on the next page. Answer the questions that follow.

1. How many major points are there in this outline? ____

2. How many supporting points are there for the first major point? ____

3. How many supporting points are there for the fifth major point? ____

4. Can you write the Roman numerals from 1 to 10?

___ ___ ___ ___ ___ ___ ___ ___ ___ ___

7. *auditory memory* (*n.phr.*) = what you remember from *hearing* something

Title

Thesis statement
I. First major point
    A. First supporting point
    B. Second supporting point
    C. Third supporting point
II. Second major point
    A. First supporting point
    B. Second supporting point
    C. Third supporting point
    D. Fourth supporting point
III. Third major point
    A. First supporting point
    B. Second supporting point
IV. Fourth major point
    A. First supporting point
    B. Second supporting point
    C. Third supporting point
V. Fifth major point
    A. First supporting point
    B. Second supporting point
Conclusion

 ACTIVITY 16 Using an outline to take notes

Master Student Tip

If you have an outline of the lecture, use it to listen for the main ideas. Use it to recognize how the details support the main ideas.

Academic students listen for the general ideas and use the specific details to support their understanding of these main ideas. This helps them recall the information in the lecture for use in class discussions, speeches, written reports, and tests. In this activity, you will use a partial outline of the lecture.

Listen to the lecture again. As you listen, try to answer the following questions:

- What is the theme of the lecture?
- What are the six major points?
- What are the minor points of each major point?

On the next page, you will see an incomplete outline of the lecture. Listen to the lecture and complete the outline. Fill in each blank with a word or phrase. You won't use all of them. Two blanks are filled in for you.

The Power of Music	

Theme: Music has the power to _move_ people.
 	
 I. Music can make people move _____.
 	
   A. _dance_ _____
 	
   B. _____
 	
   C. _____
 	
   D. _____
	access the files
	
	 clap their hands
	
	 dance ✓
	
	 move ✓
	
	 physically
	
	 sing
	
	 tap their toes

II. Music can make people move _____.
 	
   A. People don't _____.
 	
   B. _____ march together in battle.
 	
   C. Music makes workers _____.
	emotionally
	
	 know it
	
	 soldiers
	
	 stirs
	
	 work harder

III. Music can heal people when they are
 	
   A. _____.
 	
   B. _____.
 	
   C. _____.
	injured
	
	 romantic
	
	 sad
	
	 sick

IV. Music can _____ listeners.
 	
   A. Makes them _____
 	
   B. Makes them _____
 	
   C. Takes them to another _____
	entertain
	
	 excited
	
	 happy
	
	 well
	
	 world

The Power of Music (cont.)	
V. Music can _____ people	calm down
A. when they feel _____.	react
B. when they feel _____.	relax
C. when babies need to _____.	tense
	tired
VI. Music brings people _____.	focuses
A. It _____ their attention and feelings in a common experience.	makes
	stress
B. It _____ people's connections to each other _____.	stronger
	together

🎧 **ACTIVITY 17 Listening for sentences with *make***

Below and on the next page are some sentences from the lecture. Listen to the lecture again. This time, listen for sentences with make. *Fill in each blank with a word from the word list. You will use some words more than once. After you use a word, put a check (✓) by it.*

After listening to the lecture and completing all the sentences, stop the recording and look at each sentence again. Write A if a verb follows the object, or B if an adjective follows the object. The first one is done for you.

calm	fall	happy	relaxed	want ✓
calmer	feel	march	stronger	work
excited				

1. Music makes people ____*want*____ to move physically.   *A*

2. Music makes soldiers _____ together into battle.   ____

3. Music makes workers _____ harder.   ____

4. When people are sick, injured, or sad, music often _____

   makes them _____ better.

5. Does music make you _____ better? _____

6. Music makes people _____. _____

7. Music makes them _____. _____

8. Does music make you _____ good? _____

9. Does music sometimes make you _____ and

   more _____? _____

10. A lullaby makes babies _____ down and

    _____ asleep. _____

11. I don't want to make you _____ asleep right now. _____

12. Music makes people's connections to each other

    _____. _____

ACTIVITY 18 **Asking for clarification**

Successful students use many methods to get the information they need. They read and listen carefully. When they don't understand, they ask their classmates and instructor for help.

Work in groups of three. Read the questions below. Add other questions to each list. Then share them with the class.

Checking and confirming meaning

1. Did the lecturer say that music brings people together?
2. Did the teacher say *major* or *measure*?
3. So . . . people who sing together feel a strong relationship to each other. Is that right?

4. _____

5. _____

6. _____

Asking about spelling, pronunciation, grammar, or vocabulary

1. How do you spell *access*?
2. How do you pronounce M-A-J-O-R?
3. In this sentence, which part of speech is *calm*: a verb or an adjective?
4. I forgot. What's the word that means "to center your attention on something"?
5. What does *alter* mean?

6. _____

7. _____

8. _____

Asking for repetition

1. Could you say that word again, please?
2. Excuse me, would you repeat the last sentence?
3. I'm sorry. Could you speak more slowly, please?

4. _____

5. _____

6. _____

Master Student Tip

▼ Study with other students to be sure you have all the information you need. Talk with your classmates and share what you know.

⬚ Using Your Lecture Notes in Study Groups

ACTIVITY 19 **Checking your notes in a study group**

Work in groups of three. Review Activities 16 and 17. Discuss the information in your outlines and sentences. Use the questions in Activity 18 to check your understanding and to help your partners understand better.

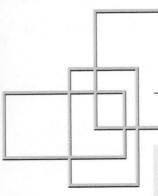

Part 2

EFFECTIVE ACADEMIC SPEAKING

In their daily academic life, students need to verbalize what they know. They often have to tell someone what they understand about a subject. The instructor gives students grades on how well they verbalize[8] their knowledge. Often, students retell parts of what they learned in a discussion and relate it to other information.

ACTIVITY 20 Retelling the content of a lecture

Work with a partner to retell the information in the lecture. Look at the main points and supporting points in your outline. You do not need to remember the lecturer's exact words, but you must remember the ideas. You may paraphrase[9] these ideas.

First Retelling

Speaker: Retell the lecture to your partner. Use your notes to remind you of the content.
Listener: Help the speaker with some keywords or ideas.
Take turns.

Second Retelling

Speaker: Retell the lecture to your partner again. This time, however, when you are the speaker, do not use your notes. Look at your listener.
Listener: Encourage and help the speaker with keywords or ideas.
Your instructor may call on you to retell some of the information in the lecture to the whole class. Get ready!

8. *verbalize* (*tr.v.*) = to use words to express your ideas
9. *paraphrase* (*tr.v.*) = to say the same thing in other words, usually to make it

ACTIVITY 21 **Checking how well you retold the lecture**

Answer the questions about yourself. Then discuss your answers with a partner.

1. Which parts of the lecture were easy for you to retell? Put a plus (+) by the easy parts.

   _____ How to access the files in the music lab and prepare for the quiz

   _____ The power of music to move people physically

   _____ The power of music to move people emotionally

   _____ The power of music to heal people

   _____ The power of music to entertain people

   _____ The power of music to relax people

   _____ The power of music to make connections among people

   Why were they easy for you to retell?

2. Look at the list above. Which parts of the lecture were difficult for you to retell? Put a minus (−) by those parts. Why were they difficult for you to retell?

3. In what ways did you and your partner help each other retell the information accurately? Put a check (✓) by all the statements that are true.

   _____ I told my partner the missing or incorrect information that I read on the outline.

   _____ I told my partner the missing or incorrect information that I recalled from my memory.

   _____ I gave my partner hints[10] about the missing or incorrect information that I read on the outline.

   _____ I gave my partner hints about the missing or incorrect information that I recalled from my memory.

   _____ I asked my partner questions about the missing or incorrect information.

   _____ My partner retold everything perfectly. I did not need to help my partner.

   _____ I retold everything perfectly. My partner did not need to help me.

10. *hint* (*n.*) = a brief or indirect suggestion, a tip

ACTIVITY **22** **Using** *make*

Compose sentences using Pattern A. Remember to use the correct form of the main verb make *and a base form verb after the object. Then practice asking and answering with a partner.*

Pattern A: Hearing popular music makes me sing.
---

1. What does a scary movie make you do?

   _____

2. What does a funny joke make you do?

   _____

3. What kind of music makes you want to dance?

   _____

4. What makes you sneeze?

   _____

5. What does cutting an onion make people do?

   _____

6. (Your own question)

   _____

   _____

Compose sentences using Pattern B.

Pattern B: Music makes me happy.

Remember to use the correct form of the verb make *and an adjective after the object. Then practice asking and answering with a partner.*

1. What kind of stories make you sad?

   _____

2. What kind of weather makes you comfortable?

_____

3. What does your mother (son, girlfriend, instructor) do that makes you happy?

_____

4. What situation makes you tense?

_____

5. What kind of exercise makes you strong?

_____

6. (Your own question)

_____

_____

Check. Did you and your partner use the correct form of the verb, e.g., make, makes, making, made?

 ACTIVITY 23 Using falling intonation on statements

> English speakers use falling intonation on statements. Our voice usually goes up on the most important word phrase in the sentence. Then it goes down at the end.

Listen to the falling intonation in these statements. The voice goes up on the keyword in the sentence. Then it goes down. Practice saying the statements. Use falling intonation.

1. Music is an important part of every culture.

2. Your body reacts in a physical way.

3. Music has the power to heal.

4. Music relaxes you when you feel tired.

ACTIVITY 24   Using rising intonation on Yes-No questions

> We generally use rising intonation on questions that have a *Yes* or a *No* answer. Our voice goes up on the most important word phrase in the sentence.

Listen to the rising intonation in these Yes-No questions. Then say them with rising intonation.

1. Is music an important part of every culture? _____

2. Do you listen to music? _____

3. Does music make you feel better? _____

4. Do you play a musical instrument? _____

Work with a partner. Ask the Yes-No questions using rising intonation. Answer the questions using falling intonation. Write your partner's answers. Take turns.

 ACTIVITY 25   Using falling intonation on Wh- questions

> We use falling intonation on questions that begin with words like *Who, What, Where, When,* and *How.* Our voice goes up on the most important word phrase in the sentence. Then it goes down at the end.

Listen to the falling intonation in these Wh- questions. Then say them with falling intonation.

1. What kind of music do you like? _____

2. When do you listen to the radio? _____

3. Who's your favorite band? _____

4. How often do you go to concerts? _____

Work with a partner. Ask the Wh- questions using falling intonation. Answer the questions using falling intonation. Write your partner's answers. Take turns.

ACTIVITY 26   Discussing likes and dislikes

> In college, instructors often require students to relate the content of a lecture or reading to their own experience. This activity helps you discuss likes and dislikes.

Read the question starters on the left and the statement starters on the right. Which express likes? Which express dislikes?

Question starters	Statement starters
_____ Do you listen to . . . ?	_____ I listen to . . .
_____ Do you like . . . ?	_____ I like . . .
_____ Do you enjoy . . . ?	_____ I enjoy . . .
_____ Are you fond of . . . ?	_____ I'm fond of . . .
_____ Are you crazy about . . . ?	_____ I love . . .
_____ Do you dislike . . . ?	_____ I'm crazy about . . .
_____ What's your favorite . . . ?	_____ I don't like . . .
_____ Who's your favorite . . . ?	_____ I dislike . . .
_____ Why do you like . . . ?	_____ I don't care for . . .
_____ Why don't you like . . . ?	_____ I can't stand . . .
_____ What kind of (music) do you like?	_____ I hate . . .
_____ How about (classical)?	_____ My favorite kind of music is . . .
_____	_____

Listen to ten short dialogues. People are talking about their musical likes and dislikes. First, listen for question starters. When you hear a question starter, write the dialogue number in the blank. Write other question starters on the last line. Listen to the dialogues again. Listen for the statement starters. When you hear a statement starter, write the dialogue number in the blank. Write other question starters on the last line.

Practice the dialogues with a partner. Monitor your intonation. Look at your partner as you speak.

1. **A:** Do you enjoy popular music?
   B: Yes, I'm crazy about pop music.

2. **A:** Do you like classical music?
   B: No, I can't stand classical.

3. **A:** What kind of music do you listen to?
   B: I love rock and roll.

4. **A:** Are you fond of jazz?
   B: I don't care for jazz music.

5. **A:** Do you dislike any kind of music?
   B: Yes, I hate country.

6. **A:** Why don't you listen to rap?
   B: Well, it's too… uh noisy.

7. **A:** What kind of music do you like?
   B: I listen to all kinds of music, but my favorite is rap.

8. **A:** Do you listen to country music?
   B: Well, yes, I sometimes listen to country.

9. **A:** Are you crazy about any kind of music?
   B: I love jazz.

10. **A:** Who is your favorite artist?
    B: My favorite? Alicia Keys. She's awesome!

ACTIVITY 27   Taking a music survey

> College students often gather opinions from different people in a *survey*.
> In this activity, you will conduct a small survey of your classmates.

Form groups of four. Write the names of your partners at the top of the following chart.[11] *Three students interview one partner at a time. Ask that partner about different music genres. Use the language from Activity 26,* Discussing likes and dislikes. *Put a check (✓) next to each different phrase that you use. As you listen, jot down the phrases each partner uses. Take turns.*

Music survey			
Kind of music	**Student**	**Student**	**Student**
Classical			
Popular			
Rock and roll			
Jazz			
Rap			
Country western			
Hip-hop			
Love songs			
Soft rock			
Hard rock			
Rhythm and blues			

11. Your instructor can get this chart on the course website to copy for use in class.

ACTIVITY 28 Following directions physically

> Most learning makes students use their minds. While instructors lecture, students listen and take notes. Some kinds of learning make students use their bodies. Students listen and perform actions. Following directions physically is an important way to master some skills. For example, dancers practice dance steps; nurses measure blood pressure; scientists do experiments, and artists paint pictures. In this activity, you will follow directions by moving physically.

▭ Circle Dance

First, you will demonstrate your listening comprehension by responding physically to directions you hear. You will participate in body learning. The whole class will stand in a circle. You will move and change partners often, according to the directions. In the end, you will use music and rhythm to guide your movements.

Listen as your instructor reads the following verb phrases without music. They are dance steps. Follow the directions by moving your body.

Get Ready

All dancers stand in a circle. (If the class is large, six or eight students may try the movements first while the rest of the class observes and claps the rhythm. If anyone in the class is uncomfortable holding hands with classmates, find another way to show partnership.)

You will find photos of the dance steps at http://esl.college.hmco.com/students.

The dance steps	How the caller may call the dance
Do #1–5 three times.	
1. CHAIN LEFT A, turn to your right and face B. B, turn to your left and face A. A and B, take each other's left hand. Walk past each other, left shoulder to left shoulder. Drop left hands.	*Chain with the left hand.* *Right Hand.* *Left Hand.* *Right Hand.* *Left Hand.* *Right.*

The dance steps	How the caller may call the dance
Take the next dancer's right hand. Walk past each other, right shoulder to right shoulder. Drop right hands. Continue. Stop. Turn and face the other way.	*Left.* *Right.* *Continue.* *Stop. Turn. Face the other way.*
2. CHAIN RIGHT Take each other's right hand. Walk past each other. Drop right hands. Take the next dancer's left hand. Walk past each other. Drop left hands. Continue. Stop. Drop hands. Turn and face the center. Join hands with the dancer to your left and the dancer to your right.	*Chain with the right hand.* *Left hand.* *Right hand.* *Left.* *Right.* *Continue.* *Stop. Join hands.* *Face the center.*
3. CIRCLE LEFT Turn to your left and walk in a big circle. Continue. Stop. (Continue to hold hands.) Face the center. Stop. Turn and go the other way.	*Circle to the left.* *Left.* *Left.* *Left.* *Continue.* *Stop. Turn. Go the other way.*
4. CIRCLE RIGHT Turn to your right and walk in a big circle. Continue. Stop. (Continue to hold hands.) Face the center.	*Circle to the right.* *Right.* *Right.* *Right.* *Continue.*
5. MIDDLE AND BACK Walk to the middle of the circle, raise your hands above your heads, and yell "Hey!" Walk back out, stretch your arms out, and yell "Yay!" Do this again.	*Walk into the middle. Hey!* *Walk back out. Yay!* *Walk into the middle. Hey!* *Walk back out. Yay!*

ACTIVITY 29   **Dancing to the music**

Now it's time to put dance steps together with music. Listen to the music and dance! Since the dance steps are repeated three times, the caller may paraphrase or shorten the sentences on the left. Follow the rhythm, and have fun!

ACTIVITY 30   **Preparing to write a report**

After students do activities like the dance you've just tried, instructors often ask students to give a written or oral report. The report may include a *reflection*, or careful and serious thought about a topic.

   The questions below ask you to reflect on your experience doing the Circle Dance. They also ask you to consider the relationship between music and other learning.

Write your responses to the questions. Then discuss them in groups of three.

1. How well did you follow the steps in the Circle Dance?

_____

_____

2. What did the music make you do? (Use *make* Pattern A. Refer to the Power Grammar on page 13.)

_____

_____

3. How did the music and movement make you feel? (Use *make* Pattern B. Refer to the Power Grammar on page 13.)

_____

_____

4. Did the music and dance create a sense of community with the class? Explain.

_____

_____

Use your notes to record an oral report of about two minutes.
Use your notes to write a report of about 200 words.

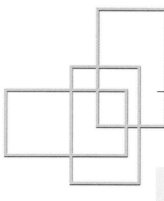

Part 3

ASSESSING YOUR LISTENING AND SPEAKING SKILLS

Some of the following questions will help you review the information about music, the theme of this chapter. Many of the questions will help you review listening and speaking skills. These types of questions may be on a test.

ACTIVITY 31 Applying skills from the chapter

Your instructor may ask you to write down the answers to the questions, discuss these questions in a group, and/or record your oral answers to the questions.

1. The lecturer presented six ways that music has the power to move people. What are the six ways?

   _____

   _____

   _____

2. In which way does music move you—personally—the most? Explain your answer.

   _____

   _____

3. What information can you find in a dictionary that can help you pronounce words more clearly?

   _____

   _____

4. How are the beats of music similar to the syllables in a word?

   _____

   _____

5. In Activities 28 and 29, you learned by doing something physically. How does this method—doing something physically—help students learn other subjects? Choose one: tennis, chemistry, nursing, English, or another subject (write it in the blank).

   _____ Explain.

   _____

   _____

6. For what kind of sentence does the voice usually rise on the most important word at the end? Give an example.

   _____

   _____

7. For what two kinds of sentences does the voice usually go up on the most important word and then go down at the end? Give two examples.

   _____

   _____

   _____

   _____

8. Without looking at Activity 26, try to recall and list five phrases to express likes and dislikes in each column below:

Question Starters	Statement Starters (likes)	Statement Starters (dislikes)
A. _____	A. _____	A. _____
B. _____	B. _____	B. _____
C. _____	C. _____	C. _____
D. _____	D. _____	D. _____
E. _____	E. _____	E. _____

ACTIVITY 32 Reviewing pronunciation, stress, and fluency

Review these words and dialogues. Write the syllable-stress code for words 1–10. Draw the final intonation over the key words in dialogues 11–14.

Then practice with a partner. Pronounce each item as clearly as you can. Have your partner listen and help you with your pronunciation of syllables and stress, and intonation. Take turns. Your instructor may ask you to record your pronunciation of these items and others in this chapter.

1. power   [___ - ___]

2. physical   [___ - ___]

3. react   [___ - ___]

4. asleep   [___ - ___]

5. nervousness   [___ - ___]

6. listener   [___ - ___]

7. relaxes   [___ - ___]

8. emotional   [___ - ___]

9. connection   [___ - ___]

10. experience   [___ - ___]

11. **A.** Is music very important?

    B. Yes, music is an important part of every culture.

12. **A.** Do you and your brother like jazz music?

    B. My brother prefers jazz music; I prefer classical music.

13. **A.** How does rock music make you feel?

    B. Rock music makes me happy. It makes me want to dance!

14. **A.** When does Mary listen to rap music?

    B. She listens to it while she cleans the house.

ACTIVITY 33 **Taking dictation**

In this dictation you will hear vocabulary and sentence patterns that you practiced in this chapter. Your instructor will tell you the number of words in each sentence. Write the number in parentheses. You will hear each sentence three times. First, listen and try to understand the meaning of the whole sentence. Second, listen and write. Third, listen and check. Use the number of words in the parentheses as a guide.

1. _____ (_____ words)
   _____

2. _____ (_____ words)
   _____

3. _____ (_____ words)
   _____

4. _____ (_____ words)
   _____

5. _____ (_____ words)
   _____

6. _____ (_____ words)
   _____

7. _____ (_____ words)
   _____

8. _____ (_____ words)
   _____

ACTIVITY 34 Summarizing your progress

How well can you perform the following objectives? Put a check (✓) in the appropriate column.

I can . . .	Barely	Somewhat	Fairly well	Very well
Use vocabulary and expressions to discuss music.				
Use a dictionary to learn the pronunciation of new academic words.				
Pronounce key vocabulary with proper syllables and word stress.				
Hear present tense endings /s/, /z/, and /ɪz/.				
Pronounce present tense endings /s/, /z/, and /ɪz/.				
Complete an outline with details.				
Use *make* sthg/sbdy + verb and *make* sthg/sbdy + adj.				
Use falling intonation on statements and Wh- questions.				
Use rising intonation on Yes-No questions.				
Ask and answer questions about likes and dislikes.				
Take dictation of sentences related to music.				

WEB POWER

You will find additional exercises related to the content in this chapter at http://esl.college.hmco.com/students.

Nutrition and Human Health

ACADEMIC FOCUS: SCIENCE ▶ NUTRITION

Academic Listening and Speaking Objectives

In this chapter, you will continue to develop your skills as an academic listener and speaker. You will hear a short lecture that an instructor gives at the beginning of a nutrition course. You will learn to pronounce academic vocabulary, and you will practice discussing topics related to food and human health. You will participate in listening, speaking, and thinking activities. In particular, you will:

- **Develop vocabulary and expressions to discuss food, nutrition, and health**
- **Use a dictionary to learn the pronunciation of new words**
- **Hear, identify, and pronounce key vocabulary with proper syllables and word stress**
- **Hear, write, and express quantities containing numbers**
- **Hear and pronounce plural noun endings /s/, /z/, and /ɪz/**
- **Repeat and rephrase information for confirmation or clarification and to enhance comprehensibility**
- **Ask questions using *How much . . . is there?* and *How many . . . are there?***
- **Ask and answer questions about food and nutrition**
- **Relate the contents of the lecture to personal food consumption**
- **Take dictation of sentences related to health and nutrition**

Part 1

⬚ Getting Ready for the Lecture

Nutrition is the science or study that deals with food and nourishment, especially in human beings. When you study nutrition, you learn how the body uses food. You learn how different foods and nutrients affect your body. With this information, you will be able to choose foods and plan your diet to improve your health while you enjoy your meals.

ACTIVITY 1 Ranking food preferences and nutritional value

Look at the illustrations. First, in each box, rank the groups of food. What kind of food do you prefer? Write 1 for your most preferred food and 4 for your least preferred food. Second, in each circle, rank the food according to its nutritional value. Write 1 for the most nutritious and 4 for the least nutritious. Third, in a group of three, discuss the kinds of food you see in each picture. Compare your rankings with your partners.

Looking at Language

In Chapter 1, you learned how to identify the number of syllables in a word by hearing and feeling the beats. You learned how to hear and feel that the stressed syllable is longer and stronger than the others. You also learned how to write the syllable-stress code. You'll continue to practice these skills in Chapter 2.

ACTIVITY 2   Identifying syllables and word stress

Listen to the pronunciation of these words. Clap or tap the number of syllables you hear. Then write the syllable-stress code. The first one is done for you. The word nutrition *has three syllables and is stressed on the second.*

1. nutrition   [_3_ ‾ _2_]   7. healthy   [___ _ ___]

2. bone   [___ - ___]   8. disease   [___ - ___]

3. human   [___ - ___]   9. examine   [___ - ___]

4. skin   [___ - ___]   10. essential   [___ - ___]

5. muscle   [___ - ___]   11. ingredient [___ - ___]

6. fat   [___ - ___]

After you mark the syllable-stress code, take turns saying the words to your partner. Pronounce each word with the correct number of syllables. Make the stressed syllable long, strong, and high. Hear and feel the beats by clapping as you pronounce. Help your partner pronounce the words with correct syllables and stress.

STRATEGY

Taking Dictation

Learning to take dictation is an important skill. Taking dictation builds and assesses[1] many language skills. Dictation can help you sharpen your listening skill, grammar ability, reading comprehension, and vocabulary knowledge, and spelling.

---

1. *assess* (*tr.v.*) = evaluates, tests, examines

🎧 **ACTIVITY 3** **Taking dictation**

You will hear the previous words in context. You will hear each sentence three times. First, listen and try to understand the meaning of the whole sentence. Second, listen and write. Third, listen and check. Use the number of words in the parentheses as a guide.

1. _____ (12 words)

   _____

2. _____ (7 words)

   _____

3. _____ (11 words)

   _____

4. _____ (6 words)

   _____

5. _____ (9 words)

   _____

6. _____ (10 words)

   _____

7. _____ (10 words)

   _____

8. _____ (6 words)

   _____

ACTIVITY 4　**Matching words with meanings**

Match each word with its definition. You will not use all of the definitions.

1. _____ bone (*n.*)

2. _____ skin (*n.*)

3. _____ muscle (*n.*)

4. _____ disease (*n.*)

5. _____ fat (*n.*)

6. _____ healthy (*adj.*)

7. _____ ingredient (*n.*)

8. _____ examine (*tr.v.*)

9. _____ essential (*adj.*)

a. A food item in a recipe.

b. A hard, white part that makes up the frame of the body, the skeleton.

c. A sickness; a condition that prevents a person or other living thing from functioning in the normal or proper way.

d. An oily white or yellow compound that is found in plant and animal tissues and that store energy.

e. A type of body tissue made of fibers that can contract and relax to cause movement or apply force.

f. In a state of good health; promoting good health.

g. The overall condition of a living thing's body and mind.

h. To observe (sbdy./sthg.) carefully; inspect or study.

i. The tissue that forms the outer covering of the body of a person or an animal; the site of the sense of touch.

j. Very important; necessary.

ACTIVITY   5   Learning the vocabulary of academic lectures

> The words in this section appear on the Academic Word List (AWL).
> You will meet these words in many academic classes. Learning these
> words will help you in your studies.

*Look up each academic word in an English dictionary. Copy the
pronunciation of each word exactly. Use the part of speech to guide you to
the right entry. Write the syllable-stress code. Study the definition. Then
compare your answers with a classmate's. The first one is done for you.*

1. assume
   (*tr.v.*)

   as·sume   ə-so͞om′   [___ - ___]

   To believe something is true without knowing.

2. affect
   (*tr.v.*)

   _____ _____   [___ - ___]

   To have an influence on (sbdy./sthg.); bring about
   a change in (sbdy./sthg.).

3. consume
   (*tr.v.*)

   _____ _____   [___ - ___]

   To eat and drink (sthg.) up.

4. effect
   (*n.*)

   _____ _____   [___ - ___]

   Something brought about by a cause or agent;
   a result.

5. energy
   (*n.*)

   _____ _____   [___ - ___]

   The power to do work or vigorous activity.

6. evident
   (*adj.*)

   _____ _____   [___ - ___]

   Easily seen or understood; obvious.

7. label
   (*n.*)

   _____ _____   [___ - ___]

   A tag or piece of paper attached to (sthg.) to
   identify it.

8. maintain
   (*tr.v.*)

   _____ _____   [___ - ___]

   To keep (sthg.) in good condition.

9. period
    (*n.*)   _____   _____   [__ - __]

    Any segment of time, long or short, that forms part
    of a longer segment and is notable for particular
    qualities or characteristics.

10. principle
    (*n.*)   _____   _____   [__ - __]

    A standard, such as a guide to behavior; a rule.

11. promote
    (*tr.v.*)   _____   _____   [__ - __]

    To aid the progress or growth of (sthg./sbdy);
    advance.

12. significant
    (*adj.*)   _____   _____   [__ - __]

    Important in effect or meaning.

13. source
    (*n.*)   _____   _____   [__ - __]

    The place where something begins.

14. structure
    (*n.*)   _____   _____   [__ - __]

    The arrangement of the tissues, organs, or other
    parts of a living thing.

15. tissue
    (*n.*)   _____   _____   [__ - __]

    A group of animal or plant cells that together
    makes up an organ that performs a certain
    function, such as nerve tissue or muscle tissue.

ACTIVITY 6 Checking and pronouncing academic words

Listen to the pronunciation of each word in the previous activity. Check the syllable-stress code.

Pronounce each word with your instructor or the recording, and then practice with a partner.

ACTIVITY 7 Listening to academic words in context

Listen to the sentences and complete each one with a word from the academic word list in the previous activity. Sometimes you will hear different forms of the words. Write the form that you hear.

1. I _____ that you are concerned about your health.

2. Have you considered the _____ of nutrition on your life?

3. A nutrient _____ growth.

4. The flavor and nutritious qualities of food _____ how people feel and act.

5. The body can remarkably renew its _____ continuously.

6. Human liver _____ can grow again if it is injured.

7. Meat, poultry, fish, dry beans, eggs, nuts, milk, yogurt, and cheese are good _____ of protein.

8. You can find _____ on clothing, machines, medications, and packaged food.

9. Carbohydrates serve as a major _____ source in the diet.

10. Vitamin C helps a person _____ healthy bones, teeth, and skin.

11. That hungry man _____ three hamburgers, two orders of French fries, and three milkshakes.

12. It is _____ that Mr. Goodman is in better health than Mr. Notwell.

13. If you consume too few nutrients over a _____ of years, you may suffer some diseases.

14. In a nutritional science class, you will learn modern nutrition _____ that you can apply to your own eating habits.

15. The food you choose has _____ effects on your body.

ACTIVITY **8** **Recognizing voiced and voiceless sounds**

In English, a sound is either *voiced* or *voiceless.* Put your hand on your throat. Put your lips together and say the sound /m/: *mmmmmm.* Can you feel your vocal cords vibrating inside your throat? Can you feel the vibration in your lips? This is a *voiced* sound. Your vocal cords vibrate for a voiced sound. In this case, your lips vibrate too!

Now say the sound /h/: *hhhhhh.* Can you feel any vibration in your throat? This is a *voiceless* sound. Your vocal cords do not vibrate for a voiceless sound.

With your instructor, pronounce only the sound at the end of each word. Then underline voiced *or* voiceless.

1. ste**p**	voiced	voiceless	7. cla**ss**	voiced	voiceless
2. fee**d**	voiced	voiceless	8. qui**z**	voiced	voiceless
3. nouri**sh**	voiced	voiceless	9. in**ch**	voiced	voiceless
4. effec**t**	voiced	voiceless	10. d**ay**	voiced	voiceless
5. maintai**n**	voiced	voiceless	11. s**ee**	voiced	voiceless
6. labe**l**	voiced	voiceless	12. sh**ow**	voiced	voiceless

Think of some other sounds in English and pronounce them. Are they voiced or voiceless?

POWER GRAMMAR

Nouns That End in –s or –es

Count nouns have singular and plural forms. In the lecture, you will hear many plural count nouns. Regular plural nouns end in –s or –es.

For example:

Some <u>nutrients</u> are water, <u>carbohydrates</u>, and <u>minerals</u>.

Your body renews its <u>structures</u> continuously.

Some <u>diseases</u> may be very serious.

    ACTIVITY 9   Listening to plural noun endings

In spoken English, the **–s** or **–es** noun endings are pronounced in three different ways, the same as the **–s** or **–es** verb endings you studied in Chapter 1.

1. If the base form ends with /s/, /z/, /ʃ/, /ʒ/, /tʃ/ or /dʒ/, the –s/es is an extra syllable /ɪz/. Examples: *classes, quizzes, wishes, garages, churches, bridges*
2. If the base form ends with with a voiceless sound /p/, /t/, /k/,[2] the –s/es is a single voiceless sound /s/. Examples: *steps, states, weeks*
3. If the base form ends with a voiced sound except /z/, /ʒ/, or /dʒ/, the –s/es is a single voiced sound /z/. Examples: *days, seas, meals, arms*.
   The most common ending sound is /z/.

2. and sometimes /f/ and /Θ/

Listen to the singular form and the plural forms of the following nouns.

Base form	Voiceless /s/	Base form	Voiced /z/	Base form	Extra syllable /ɪz/
effect	effects	arm	arms	class	classes
fact	facts	bone	bones	source	sources
nutrient	nutrients	day	days	disease	diseases
product	products	kind	kinds	quiz	quizzes
step	steps	label	labels	exercise	exercises
group	groups	leg	legs	phrase	phrases
week	weeks	meal	meals		
		mineral	minerals		
		muscle	muscles		
		pound	pounds		
		principle	principles		
		protein	proteins		
		quality	qualities		
		structure	structures		
		tissue	tissues		
		vitamin	vitamins		
		word	words		
		year	years		

Pronounce each pair of words with your instructor or the recording. Then practice with a partner.

ACTIVITY 10 Listening to and pronouncing numbers

> In many lectures, you will hear numbers to describe amounts. When you describe items, you will often use numbers, too.

Listen to these numbers and underline the stressed syllables. The first one is done for you.

Numerals	Words
17	seven<u>teen</u>
70	seventy
14	fourteen
40	forty
341	three hundred forty-one, or three hundred and forty-one
9,210	nine thousand two hundred ten, or nine thousand two hundred and ten
1,500	one thousand five hundred, or fifteen hundred
4,002	four thousand two, or four thousand and two
35,900	thirty-five thousand nine hundred
280,000	two hundred eighty thousand
3,000,000	three million
3,500,000	three million five hundred thousand, or three point five million
700 or 800	seven or eight hundred

Pronounce each pair of words with your instructor or the recording and then practice with a partner.

ACTIVITY **11** **Listening to numbers in context**

Listen to the sentences and circle the numbers you hear.

1. A banana contains about (109 190 1090 1009) calories.

2. A healthy diet includes (5 6 5–6 56) servings of fruit or vegetables each day.

3. An average person needs to eat (2,000 2,500 2,000–2,500 20,000–25,000) calories a day.

4. Human beings have known about the medical properties of plants for over (20 2,000 20,000 200,000) years.

5. Researchers studied the eating habits of (1,146 11,456 11,546 11,000,456) health-conscious people.

6. This pill contains (75 715 750 750,000) milligrams of calcium.

7. You'll consume about (100 1,000 100,000 1,000,000) pounds of food in your lifetime.

8. Can you imagine eating (17,157 71,175 71,157 70,157) meals?

9. At the beginning of the previous century, Americans chose from among (5 500 5,000 50,000) or so different foods.

10. Today, Americans choose from more than (5 500 5,000 50,000) different foods.

▭ Getting Information from the Lecture

Students listen to their instructors to learn facts and to get information that will help them learn. You will listen to the lecture several times. Each time you will listen for a specific purpose.

 ACTIVITY 12 Listening for questions

Your instructor will play the lecture for you. As you listen to the lecture for the first time, listen for questions. Raise your hand each time you hear the lecturer ask a question. Your instructor will model this activity for the first few questions.

A lecturer makes many statements to give information. In addition, some lecturers ask questions to help listeners focus on the important points.

ACTIVITY 13 **Focusing on questions**

You will hear the lecture again. Listen for questions about nutrition. Jot down the questions about nutrition in the question (Q) column. (Do not write all of the questions.) You do not need to write the exact question. Write the most important words. Your instructor will model this for you.

Q	A

ACTIVITY 14 **Focusing on answers**

Listen to the lecture again. This time jot down answers to the questions in the answer (A) column. You do not need to write the exact answer. Write the keywords.

POWER GRAMMAR

Numbers and Plural Nouns

In a noun phrase, the articles *a* and *an* and the number *one* (1) are followed by a singular noun: *a meal, an egg, one person.* Any number larger than one is followed by a plural noun. There may be other words that modify the noun in the phrase.

For example:

365 <u>days</u>

2,000–2,500 <u>calories</u>

750 <u>milligrams</u> of calcium

5-6 <u>servings</u> of fruit or vegetables

11,456 health-conscious <u>people</u>

 ACTIVITY 15   **Listening for number phrases**

In Activities 10 and 11, you practiced listening to numbers individually and in sentences. Listen to the first part of the lecture again. This time listen for number phrases such as 109 calories *or* 50,000 different foods. *Write down each number phrase you hear. The first one is done for you.*

1. <u>3 meals/day</u>

2. _____

3. _____

4. _____

5. _____

6. _____

7. _____

8. _____

9. _____

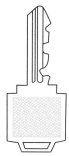

 **STRATEGY**

Listening for Keywords

Keywords are usually repeated many times during a lecture because they are important. Because this lecture is an introduction to a nutrition class, you often will hear the words *nutrient*, *nourish* and others in the same word families.

ACTIVITY 16 Listening for repeated keywords

Listen to the third part of the lecture again. Your instructor may ask you to do one of the following:

- Each time you hear a word from this word family, raise your hand and call out each word you hear.
- Each time you hear a word from this word family, write the word in the blanks.

nutrient	nutrients	nutrition	nutritious
nourish	nourishes	nourishing	nourishment

1. _____   5. _____

2. _____   6. _____

3. _____   7. _____

4. _____   8. _____

▭ Using Your Notes to Answer Questions

ACTIVITY 17 Comprehending the lecture

Listen to eight statements about the lecture. Refer to your notes in Activities 12–15 and your auditory memory. After listening to each statement, circle True or False according to your information.

1. True   False

2. True   False

3. True   False

4. True   False

5. True   False

6. True   False

7. True   False

8. True   False

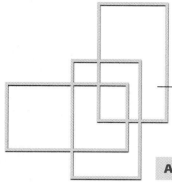

Part 2

ACTIVITY 18 Retelling the content of the lecture

Suppose your classmate missed a lecture in your class. You can help your classmate by retelling the main points of the lecture. Retelling also helps you review and remember what you learned.

Work with a partner to retell the information in the lecture. Look at your notes for Activities 12–16, where you focused on questions, answers, number phrases, and keywords. You do not need to remember the lecturer's exact words, but you must remember the ideas. Paraphrase these ideas.

First Retelling

Speaker: Retell the lecture to your partner. Use your notes to remind you of the content.

Listener: Help the speaker with some keywords or ideas.

Take turns.

Second Retelling

Speaker: Retell the lecture to your partner again. Do not use your notes. Look at your listener and retell from memory.

Listener: Encourage and help the speaker with some keywords or ideas.

Take turns. Your instructor may call on you to retell the information in the lecture to the whole class. Get ready!

ACTIVITY 19 Checking how well you retold the lecture

Answer the questions about yourself. Then discuss your answers with a partner.

1. Which parts of the lecture were easy for you to retell? Put a plus (+) by the easy parts.

   _____ The importance of a nutritious breakfast

   _____ The amount of food people eat in a lifetime

   _____ The effects of the food on your body

   _____ How the body renews its structures continuously

   _____ The meaning of nutrients and examples of nutrients

   _____ The way that your choice of foods influences your health

   Why were they easy for you to retell?

2. Look at the list above. Which parts of the lecture were difficult for you to retell? Put a minus (−) by the difficult parts.

   Why were they difficult for you to retell?

3. In what ways did you and your partner help each other retell the information accurately? Put a check (✓) by all the statements that are true.

   _____ I told my partner the missing or incorrect information that I read in my exercises on questions, answers, number phrases, and key words.

   _____ I told my partner the missing or incorrect information that I recalled from my memory.

   _____ I gave my partner hints about the missing or incorrect information that I read in my notes.

   _____ I gave my partner hints about the missing or incorrect information that I recalled from my memory.

   _____ I asked my partner questions about the missing or incorrect information.

   _____ My partner retold everything perfectly. I did not need to help my partner.

   _____ I retold everything perfectly. My partner did not need to help me.

Learning to Ask for Clarification

To be a good listener in a conversation, you need to understand what the speaker is saying—you want confirmation. Sometimes you are not sure you got the information right—you need clarification. You can ask for confirmation or clarification in several ways. One way is to repeat the speaker's exact words. Another way is to rephrase the speaker's idea. Still another way is to ask if you heard the speaker correctly.

ACTIVITY 20   Asking for confirmation and clarification

Who's talking about what? What information needs clarification? Listen to four dialogues without reading the script. Jot down notes in the chart below. Discuss your notes with the class.

	Who	Where	Topic	Info for confirmation or clarification
1				
2				
3				
4				

> Speakers repeat information with falling intonation when they are fairly sure the information is correct. They use rising intonation when they need confirmation or clarification.

Using intonation for confirmation and clarification. *Listen to the dialogues again. Draw a rising or falling arrow over each phrase in bold. Then talk about the meanings.*

	Intonation notes
1. A = a student B = a records technician	
A: I'd like a copy of my grade record, please. **B:** May I have your student ID number? **A:** Yes. It's 4-3-2... **B: 4-3-2...** **A:** 1-1-2-9. **B:** That's 4-3-2 ... **1-1-2-9?** **A:** Yes, that's correct. **B:** Okay. I'll be right back.	*Falling (sure)* *Rising (not sure, wants confirmation)*
2. A = a doctor at the student health center B = a student	Intonation notes
A: Here, Mamie. Take two of these pills three times a day, with a full cup of water. **B:** Excuse me. Take **three pills two times a day**? **A:** Take two pills three times a day. Two at breakfast, two at lunch, and two at dinner. **B:** Oh, I see. Two pills, at three meals. With **coffee**? **A:** No, just drink **water**, eight ounces of **water**. Caffeine will make the medication lose its effect. **B:** Okay, a cup of water. **A:** That's right. If you have any problems, just give me a call. **B:** Thank you, doctor.	

3. A = a professor, during class B = a student	Intonation notes
A: And the most important nutrient for the human body is H_2O. **B:** Excuse me, uh, H_2O? **A:** H_2O? Oh, H_2O means water. H2 stands for two atoms of hydrogen, and O stands for oxygen. Each molecule of water is composed of two hydrogen atoms and one oxygen atom. **B:** Thank you.	

4. A = a student, during an office hour B = a professor	Intonation notes
A: Professor Wood, I'm almost done with my project, but ... well, I'm sorry, I won't be able to take the final exam because I have a family emergency ... my grandmother is very sick ... I have to leave tomorrow. I do want to finish the class, though. **B:** I'm sorry to hear that. Well, I'll have to fill out an incomplete form ... Let me write in your name ... It's Gary Lopez, right? **A:** Yes. **B:** Gary **L-O-P-E-Z**? **A:** My last name is spelled with an S; it's L-O-P-E-S. **B:** **L-O-P-E-S**. And it's for Nutrition 1 ... and now I need your student ID number. **A:** It's 3-4-5-7-8-1-9-0-7-8. **B:** Is that **3-4-5, 7-8-1, 5-0-7-8**? **A:** Sorry. Not quite. It's 3-4-5, 7-8-1, <u>9</u>-0-7-8. **B:** Okay, ... <u>9</u>-0-7-8. You're all set. You know you have a year to complete the project and the final. **A:** I will, Professor Wood. As soon as I get back, I'll contact you. **B:** Good luck. **A:** Thank you very much.	

Repeat the dialogs after your instructor or the recording. Then practice them with a partner. Pay attention to rising and falling intonation.

ACTIVITY 21 Hearing fourteen or forty

> Numbers such as fourteen and eighteen are usually stressed on the second syllable, and we pronounce the "t" with a voiceless sharp puff of air. Numbers such as forty and eighty are stressed on the first syllable, and we usually pronounce the "t" as a voiced sound, somewhat like /d/.

Listen to these numbers and then pronounce them.

The "teen" numbers	The "ten" numbers
13 thirteen	30 thirty
14 fourteen	40 forty
15 fifteen	50 fifty
16 sixteen	60 sixty
17 seventeen	70 seventy
18 eighteen	80 eighty
19 nineteen	90 ninety

Practice with a partner. Use the following dialogue as a model.

Say any number from the lists above.

A: 13.

Ask a question using the teen and the ten number.

B: Did you say 13 or 30?

Tell which one you didn't say. Tell which one you said.

A: I didn't say 30. I said 13.

Confirm the number.

B: You said 13, right?

Agree.

A: That's right.

ACTIVITY 22   Saying number phrases and abbreviations

In presenting facts, students often need to quantify information, or tell the amounts. Abbreviations are short forms: *mi = mile(s), hr = hour(s)*. You will often read abbreviations on labels or notes that instructors write on the board. When you speak, you usually need to say the long form. You need to be able to express numbers and measurements accurately.

Discuss the meanings and abbreviations of the following measurements. Then listen to the number phrases and repeat them.

Abbreviations	Spoken Form
50 mg.	fifty milligrams
5.5 g.	five point five grams
412 cal.	four hundred twelve calories
1/2 oz.	one-half ounce (a half ounce, half an ounce)
1/4 tsp.	one-fourth teaspoon (a fourth, one quarter, a quarter)
2 T.	two tablespoons
3/4 c.	three fourths of a cup (three quarters cup)
39%	thirty-nine percent
< 20%	less than twenty percent
> 50 g.	more than fifty grams
6–11 svg/d	six to eleven servings a day (per day)
32° F.	thirty-two degrees Fahrenheit
100° C.	one hundred degrees Celsius

ACTIVITY 23 **Stressing content words**

In spoken English, some words are stressed and other words are unstressed. Stressed words are long, strong, and high. When we speak, we stress the *content words.*[3] In contrast, we don't usually stress *function words.*[4] They are short, weak, and low.

Listen to the following sentences. The content words are marked in bold, and the stressed syllables are in capitals. Say the content words long, strong, and high. The function words are marked in gray. Say the function words short, weak, and low.

1. **START** your **DAY**.

2. **START** your **DAY** with **BREAK**fast.

3. a **GOOD** nu**TRI**tious **BREAK**fast

4. It's im**POR**tant to **START** your **DAY** with **BREAK**fast.

5. It's im**POR**tant to **START** your **DAY** with a **GOOD** nu**TRI**tious **BREAK**fast.

Work with a partner. Underline the content words in the following paragraph.

How many calories should a person consume? Let's consider two examples. A woman is twenty years old. She stands five feet five inches tall. She weighs about one hundred twenty-eight pounds. She has an average amount of body fat. She engages in light activity. She should consume about two thousand, two hundred calories per day. Here's a second example. A man is twenty years old. He stands five feet ten inches tall. He weighs one hundred sixty pounds. He has an average amount of body fat. He engages in light activity. He needs an intake of about two thousand nine hundred calories. These are only simple examples. In fact nobody is average. People's energy needs vary greatly.

Listen to the model and check your answers. Then practice the sentences with a partner.

---

3. *content word* (*n. phr.*) = a word that gives the most information in a sentence. These include nouns, main verbs, adjectives, and adverbs.
4. *function word* (*n. phr.*) = a word that shows a grammatical relationship but does not have much meaning by itself. These words include articles, prepositions, conjunctions, auxiliary verbs, and pronouns.

ACTIVITY 24   Exchanging and confirming information

> Both the speaker and the listener are responsible for successful communication. In this activity, you will practice giving and receiving information that uses quantities, or number phrases. You will also practice asking for confirmation and clarification. After you ask and your partner confirms the information, write it down. Use abbreviations.

Discuss the model dialogue with your class.

Dialogue	Ask	B's Notes (progressive)
A: Water boils at 212 degrees.		
B: Excuse me, at how many degrees?	✓	*Water boils*
A: Two hundred twelve.		
B: Is that Fahrenheit or Celsius?	✓	*Water boils – 212°*
A: Fahrenheit. 212 degrees Fahrenheit.		
B: I got it. Water boils at two hundred twelve degrees Fahrenheit.	✓	*Water boils – 212° F.*
A: Right.		
B: Thank you.		
A: You're welcome.		

Your instructor will tell you a sentence with number phrases. Listen and ask four questions for confirmation or clarification. Put a check in the box when you ask a question. After your instructor confirms each quantity, write down the information.

☐ ☐ ☐ ☐ _____

Now you are ready to practice with a partner. Decide who is Partner A and who is Partner B. Partner A, turn to the next page. Partner B, turn to Appendix page 259.

Partner A

Partner B: turn to Appendix page 260. You and your partner will take turns speaking, listening, and confirming information about nutrition and health.

Partner A: Read sentence 1. Partner B: Listen, ask one or more questions for clarification or confirmation.

Partner A: Respond to Partner B's questions. Partner B: take notes.

Partner B: Read sentence 1. Partner A: Listen, ask one or more questions for clarification or confirmation.

Partner B: Respond to Partner A's questions. Partner A: take notes.

Partner A: Read sentence 2, and so on.

Partner B: Read sentence 2, and so on.

Continue taking turns in this way until you finish or until your instructor tells you to stop.

Partner A: Read one sentence at a time to Partner B. Use the words in parentheses to help you pronounce the numbers.

1. A human body has 206 (two hundred and six) bones.
2. There are 16 (sixteen) grams of fiber in a cup of dried beans.
3. That turkey sandwich contains about 294 (two hundred ninety-four) calories.
4. We should eat 5 to 12 (five to twelve) servings of grain products per day.
5. An average person should consume 15 to 20 (fifteen to twenty) percent calories from protein.
6. Here are some typical servings of fruit: one medium apple, half a grapefruit, $^3/_4$ (three quarters) cup of juice, $^1/_2$ (a half) cup of canned fruit, and $^1/_4$ (one-fourth) cup of dried fruit.

Confirm   My partner's number phrases

1. ☐ _____

2. ☐ _____

3. ☐ _____

4. ☐ _____

5. ☐ _____

6. ☐ _____

ACTIVITY 25   Checking your communication strategies

Answer the following questions after completing Activity 24, page 64 and Appendix page 259.

1. As a listener, how many questions did you ask your partner about her or his information? _____

2. As a speaker, how many times did you repeat or confirm your information? _____

3. As a speaker, which information was the easiest for you to <u>say</u> to your partner? _____

4. As a listener, which information was the easiest for you to <u>understand</u> from your partner? _____

5. Ask your instructor questions about items that are unclear to you.

_____

POWER GRAMMAR

How Much and *How Many*

<u>*How much* + noncount noun</u>

Words like *water*, *calcium*, and *cholesterol* are noncount nouns. They are used in the singular form. When we ask a question about quantity, we use *How much . . . ?*

For example:

How much water do you drink every day?

<u>*How many* + plural count noun</u>

Words like *banana*, *calorie*, and *serving* are count nouns. They are used in both the singular form and the plural form, for example *one banana, – two bananas*. When we ask a question about quantity, we use *How many* with the plural noun form:

For example:

How many bananas are there?

ACTIVITY **26** Using *How much* and *How many*?

Look at the two patterns in the boxes. Work with a partner to complete each question with much *or* many. *Add* -s *or* -es *to plural count nouns. Use your dictionary to look up the meaning of unfamiliar words.*

How much [singular noncount noun] is there?	How many [plural count noun] are there?

1. How _____ calcium _____ there?

2. How _____ calorie _____ there?

3. How _____ cholesterol _____ there?

4. How _____ cup _____ there?

5. How _____ fat _____ there?

6. How _____ fiber _____ there?

7. How _____ gram _____ there?

8. How _____ iron _____ there?

9. How _____ nutrient _____ there?

10. How _____ ounce _____ there?

11. How _____ sodium _____ there?

12. How _____ Vitamin A _____ there?

13. How _____ serving _____ there?

14. How _____ milligram _____ there?

15. How _____ Vitamin C _____ there?

ACTIVITY 27 Understanding nutrition facts on labels

On any packaged food container, there is a Nutrition Facts label. This shows the nutrient contents of the food. By reading the Nutrition Facts labels, consumers can get nutrition information about almost every food on a grocery shelf.

Match the information below with an example on the label.

1. Each label shows a standard serving size at the top. This serving size allows consumers to make nutritional comparisons of similar products. Some common units are cup, tablespoon, teaspoon, piece, slice, and fraction (such as "¼ pizza"). The number of servings per container is shown below the serving size.

2. The middle portion of a Nutrition Facts label shows information about the amount per serving of calories and certain nutrients. Some of these nutrients are fat, cholesterol, sodium, carbohydrates, protein, Vitamin A and calcium. Other nutrients of major health concern are also shown. The content of the middle section is different for different kinds of food.

3. The top and middle portions of the label show the Nutrition Facts specifically for the food in the package.

4. The bottom portion of the label shows the Daily Values. Daily Values (DV) are nutrient standards used on all food labels. They are the same on all labels.[5]

5. Nutrition labels express nutrients as a percentage of Daily Values (DVs) for a 2,000-calorie diet. This label is from The U.S. Food and Drug Administration's web page *The Food Label* http://www.fda.gov/opacom/backgrounders/foodlabel/newlabel.html

Sample Nutrition Facts Label

Nutrition Facts

Serving Size ½ cup (114 g)
Servings Per Container 4

Amount Per Serving
Calories 90   Calories from Fat 30

	% Daily Value*
Total Fat 3 g	5%
Saturated Fat 0 g	0%
Cholesterol 0 mg	0%
Sodium 300 mg	13%
Total Carbohydrates 13 g	4%
Dietary Fiber 3 g	12%
Sugars 3 g	
Protein 3 g	

Vitamin A 80%	•	Vitamin C 60%
Calcium 4%	•	Iron 4%

*Percent Daily Values are based on a 2,000 calorie diet. Your daily values may be higher or lower depending on your calorie needs:

		Calories	2,000	2,500
Total Fat	Less than		85 g	80 g
Sat. Fat	Less than		20 g	25 g
Cholesterol	Less than		300 mg	300 mg
Sodium	Less than		2,400 g	2,400 g
Total Carbohydrates			300 g	375 g
Dietary Fiber			25 g	30 g

Calories per gram:
Fat 9 • Carbohydrates 4 • Protein 4

ACTIVITY 28 **Asking questions about nutrition labels**

Unscramble each group of words to make a question. Capitalize the first word, and end the sentence with a question mark. Refer to the nutrition facts label in Activity 27. All of the questions except one use the patterns in the box. Which question is different? _____ After writing the questions, answer each question in a complete sentence.

> How much/many [noun 1] is/are there per/in one [noun 2]?
> How much/many [noun 1] does one [noun 2] contain?
> How much/many [noun 1] come(s) from [noun 2]?
> How much of the Daily Value of [noun 1] is provided by [noun 2]?

1. servings are container how many per there

    Q. _____

    A. _____

2. are calories how in many one serving there

    Q. _____

    A. _____

3. calories come many fat from how

    Q. _____

    A. _____

4. fat contain does how one much serving total

    Q. _____

    A. _____

5. cholesterol how in is much one serving there

    Q. _____

    A. _____

6. sodium much contain does how one serving

    Q. _____

    A. _____

7. daily value how is much of of one provided by serving the Vitamin A

Q. _____

A. _____

8. serving what is size the

Q. _____

A. _____

With a partner, practice asking and answering the questions with good stress and intonation. Pronounce the content words long and the function words short.

ACTIVITY 29 **Asking about facts on nutrition labels**

With a partner, ask and answer questions about the contents and nutritional values of the following products. Use the question and answer patterns in Activity 28.

Hot Chili with Beans

Ingredients: Tomatoes, beef, water, beans, dehydrated onions, flavoring, jalapeño peppers, modified food starch, paprika, salt, dehydrated bell peppers, sugar, chile de arbol flavor (contains soybean oil and paprika) vinegar, dehydrated habanero peppers.

Nutrition Facts

Serving Size 1 cup (247 g)
Servings Per Container about 2

Amount Per Serving
Calories 340   Calories from Fat 150

	% Daily Value*
Total Fat 17 g	**26%**
Saturated Fat 7 g	**35%**
Cholesterol 45 mg	**15%**
Sodium 870 mg	**36%**
Total Carbohydrate 31 g	**10%**
Dietary Fiber 6 g	**24%**
Sugars 7 g	
Protein 17 g	

Vitamin A 10%	•	Vitamin C 0%
Calcium 6%	•	Iron 15%

*Percent Daily Values are based on a 2,000 calorie diet. Your daily values may be higher or lower depending on your calorie needs:

		Calories	2,000	2,500
Total Fat	Less than		65 g	80 g
Sat. Fat	Less than		20 g	25 g
Cholesterol	Less than		300 mg	300 mg
Sodium	Less than		2,400 mg	2,400 mg
Total Carbohydrates			300 mg	375 mg
Dietary Fiber			25 g	30 g

Calories per gram: Fat 0 = Carbohydrates 4 + Protein 4

Trail Mix

Ingredients: Salted roasted peanuts, raisins, M&M's® plain chocolate candies, almonds, cashews—Peanuts roasted in peanut oil and salt, raisins coated in partially hydrogenated cottonseed oil and soybean oil, M&M's plain chocolate, candies (sugar, chocolate, cocoa butter, skim milk, milkfat, lactose, soy lecithin, salt, artificial flavors), sugar, cornstarch, less than 1% corn syrup, gum acacia coloring (includes Red #40 Lake, Yellow #6, Blue #2 Lake, Yellow #5, Blue #1 Lake, Red #40, Blue #1), and dextrin, almonds roasted in canola and almond or safflower oil and salt, cashews roasted in peanut oil and salt.

Nutrition Facts

Serving Size 3 Tablespoons (30 g)
Servings Per Container About 15

Amount Per Serving
Calories 148   Calories from Fat 64

	% Daily Value*
Total Fat 7 g	11%
Saturated Fat 2 g	9%
Cholesterol 0 mg	0%
Sodium 39 mg	1%
Total Carbohydrate 16 g	6%
Dietary Fiber 2 g	8%
Sugars 7 g	
Protein 4 g	

Vitamin A 0%	•	Vitamin C 0%
Calcium 11%	•	Iron 3%

*Percent Daily Values are based on a 2,000 calorie diet. Your daily values may be higher or lower depending on your calorie needs:

		Calories	2,000	2,500
Total Fat	Less than		65 g	80 g
Sat. Fat	Less than		20 g	25 g
Cholesterol	Less than		300 g	300 g
Sodium	Less than		2,400 g	2,400 g
Total Carbohydrates			300 mg	375 mg
Dietary Fiber			25 g	30 g

Calories per gram: Fat 0 = Carbohydrates 4 + Protein 4

ACTIVITY 30 **Presenting information about a food you eat**

Choose one kind of food that you like to eat. Bring to class the Nutrition Facts label of this food. Prepare a short talk (four to five minutes) about its nutritional value. Use number phrases. Pay attention to count and noncount nouns. Pronounce regular plural count nouns with /s/, /z/, and /ɪz/ endings. Be ready to answer questions about your food.

Being a timekeeper

One student in each group should use a watch or clock to keep the speaker's time. The time keeper may hold up one finger for each minute of speech. For a short talk of four to five minutes, the speaker should conclude the presentation between the fourth and fifth finger.

Form a group of four students. Take turns speaking and listening. Take turns being the time keeper.

Speaker: Show your partners your nutrition facts label. Tell why you chose to present this food. Talk about the contents and nutritional value of your food. As you speak, remember to use proper vocabulary, grammar, and pronunciation.

Listeners: Repeat the speaker's key information to confirm your understanding. Ask questions for clarification. Take brief notes in the chart below.

Timekeeper: Hold up your fingers to show how long the speaker has talked. Take notes with your other hand if possible.

Partner's name			
Product			
Serving Size			
Servings			
Calories per serving			
Total Fat			
Cholesterol			
Total Carbohydrate			
Sodium			
Protein			
Vitamin A			
Vitamin C			

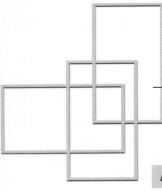

Part 3

ASSESSING YOUR LISTENING
AND SPEAKING SKILLS

ACTIVITY 31 **Applying skills from the chapter**

Some of the following questions will help you review the information about nutrition, the theme of this chapter. Many of the questions will help you review listening and speaking skills. These types of questions may be on a test.

Your instructor may ask you to write down the answers to the questions, discuss these questions in a group, and/or record your oral answers to the questions.

1. The lecturer presented many ideas. What are two ideas from the lecture that are important to human nutrition and health?

_____

_____

_____

2. Is it important to read food labels? What can you learn from looking at food labels?

_____

_____

_____

3. When you listen for questions in a lecture, how can this help you hear important information?

_____

_____

_____

4. When you retell the content of a lecture, how can this help you and other students?

   _____

   _____

   _____

5. When you ask someone for confirmation or clarification, how can this help your communication?

   _____

   _____

   _____

6. When should you use *how much* and when should you use *how many*? Explain your answer, and give two examples of each.

   _____

   _____

   _____

   _____

7. When should you use /s/, /z/, and /ɪz/ endings? Explain your answer, and give two examples of each.

   _____

   _____

   _____

   _____

8. What is the difference between repeating information with falling intonation ↘ and repeating information with rising intonation? ↗ Compare the two dialogues on the next page, and explain the difference in meaning.

   _____

   _____

   _____

Dialogue 1
A: My last name is Byrd.

B: Byrd.

Dialogue 2
A: My last name is Byrd.

B: Byrd?

_____

_____

_____

ACTIVITY 32 **Reviewing pronunciation, stress, and fluency**

Review these words and dialogues. Write the syllable stress code for words 1–14. Draw the final intonation over the keywords in dialogs 15–16. Then practice with a partner. Pronounce each item as clearly as you can. Have your partner listen and help you with your pronunciation of syllables, stress, and intonation. Take turns. Practice several times to develop fluency. Your instructor may ask you to record your pronunciation of these items and others in this chapter.

1. assume   [___ - ___]   8. period   [___ - ___]

2. consume   [___ - ___]   9. principle   [___ - ___]

3. energy   [___ - ___]   10. promote   [___ - ___]

4. evident   [___ - ___]   11. significant [___ - ___]

5. individual [___ - ___]   12. source   [___ - ___]

6. maintain   [___ - ___]   13. structure [___ - ___]

7. major   [___ - ___]   14. tissue   [___ - ___]

15. **A.** How many children attend the physical exercise class on Mondays?

   B. Fifteen boys and forty girls.

16. **A.** How much sugar is there in those peanuts?

   B. These peanuts? These peanuts contain 2 grams of sugar.

ACTIVITY 33 **Taking dictation**

In this dictation you will hear vocabulary and sentence patterns that you practiced in this chapter. Your instructor will tell you the number of words in each sentence. You will hear each sentence three times. First, listen and try to understand the meaning of the whole sentence. Second, listen and write. Third, listen and check. Use the number of words in the parentheses as a guide.

1. _____ (____ words)

   _____

2. _____ (____ words)

   _____

3. _____ (____ words)

   _____

4. _____ (____ words)

   _____

5. _____ (____ words)

   _____

6. _____ (____ words)

   _____

7. _____ (____ words)

   _____

8. _____ (____ words)

   _____

ACTIVITY 34 Summarizing your progress

How well can you perform the following objectives?

I can ...	Barely	Somewhat	Fairly well	Very well
Use vocabulary and expressions to discuss food and nutrition.				
Use a dictionary to learn the pronunciation of new academic words.				
Pronounce key vocabulary with proper syllables and word stress.				
Express quantities containing numbers.				
Hear plural noun endings /s/, /z/, and /ɪz/.				
Pronounce plural noun endings /s/, /z/, and /ɪz/.				
Repeat information for confirmation and clarification.				
Ask questions using *How much* and *How many*.				
Ask and answer questions about food and nutrition.				
Relate the contents of the lecture to my own choice of food.				
Take dictation of sentences related to health and nutrition.				

WEB POWER

You will find additional exercises related to the content in this chapter at http://esl.college.hmco.com/students.

Themes
of Geography

ACADEMIC FOCUS:
SOCIAL SCIENCE ▶ GEOGRAPHY

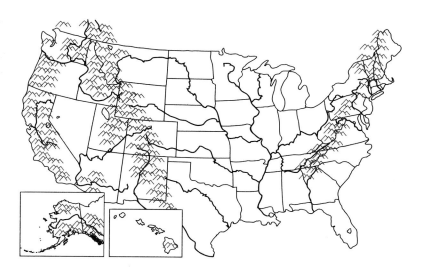

Academic Listening and Speaking Objectives

In this chapter, you will develop your skills as an academic listener and speaker in the discipline of geography. You will hear a short lecture that an instructor gives at the beginning of a physical geography course. You will pronounce academic vocabulary and practice discussing topics related to physical geography. You will participate in listening, speaking, and thinking activities. In particular, you will:

- ▓ **Develop vocabulary and expressions to discuss geography**
- ▓ **Use a dictionary to learn the pronunciation of new words**
- ▓ **Recognize transitions that identify important points**
- ▓ **Understand the relationship of main ideas and examples**
- ▓ **Hear, locate, and pronounce cities in the United States**
- ▓ **Talk about information on a map**
- ▓ **Ask choice questions with proper intonation**
- ▓ **Ask (and answer) questions using *east*, *west*, *north*, and *south***
- ▓ **Ask questions using *How far* and *How long***
- ▓ **Discuss the geography of your local area**
- ▓ **Take dictation of sentences related to geography**

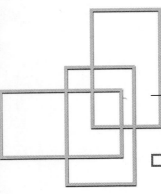

Part 1

EFFECTIVE ACADEMIC LISTENING

🔲 Getting Ready for the Lecture

Geography is the study of all the physical features of the earth's surface, including its climate and the distribution of plant, animal, and human life. When you study geography, you learn about the physical features of a place or region, for example, mountains, rivers, and deserts.

ACTIVITY 1 Studying basic landforms

A landform is a natural physical feature of the earth's surface.

With a partner, look at the illustration and locate the following natural landforms.

1. mountain — A raised portion of the earth's surface, generally very large and rising to a great height.
2. valley — A long narrow area of low land between hills or mountains.
3. prairie — A large, level area of grassland without trees, especially in central North America.
4. desert — A dry area with little rainfall and where few plants grow.
5. island — A land mass that is completely surrounded by water.
6. lake — A large body of water surrounded by land.
7. peninsula — A narrow piece of land that is nearly surrounded by water, but connected to the mainland.
8. ocean — The entire body of saltwater covering more than 70 percent of the earth's surface.
9. river — A large body of water that moves in one direction toward an ocean or lake.
10. waterfall — Water falling from a high place.

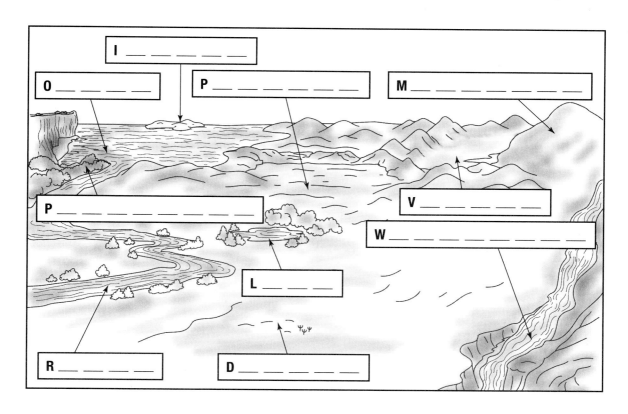

I _ _ _ _ _ _

O _ _ _ _

P _ _ _ _ _ _ _

M _ _ _ _ _ _ _ _

P _ _ _ _ _ _ _ _ _ _

V _ _ _ _ _ _

W _ _ _ _ _ _ _ _

L _ _ _ _

R _ _ _ _ _

D _ _ _ _ _ _

ACTIVITY 2 Listing largest to smallest

Work in a group of three students. List the following types of land areas in order of largest to smallest. Use your knowledge of the United States. Then use your knowledge of this country to name three of each.

| city | state | country | county | continent |

Largest _____ > _____ > _____ > _____ > _____ Smallest

Looking at Language

 **ACTIVITY 3** Identifying syllables and word stress

Listen to the pronunciation of these words. Clap or tap the number of syllables you hear. Then write the syllable-stress code. The first one is done for you.

1. absolute   [_3_ - _3_]
2. characteristic [___ - ___]
3. especially   [___ - ___]
4. explore   [___ - ___]
5. geographer   [___ - ___]
6. liberty   [___ - ___]
7. origin   [___ - ___]
8. refer   [___ - ___]
9. variety   [___ - ___]
10. weather   [___ - ___]

After you mark the syllable-stress code, take turns saying the words to your partner. Pronounce each word with the correct number of syllables. Make the stressed syllable long, strong, and high. Hear and feel the beats by clapping as you pronounce. Help your partner pronounce the words with correct syllables and stress.

STRATEGY

Learning about Dictation

As you recall, taking dictation can help you sharpen your listening skill, grammar ability, reading comprehension, vocabulary knowledge, and spelling.

ACTIVITY 4 **Taking dictation**

You will hear the words in Activity 3 in context. You will hear each sentence three times. First, listen and try to understand the meaning of the whole sentence. Second, listen and write. Third, listen and check. Use the number of words in the parentheses as a guide.

1. _____ (8 words)

   _____

2. _____ (10 words)

   _____

3. _____ (10 words)

   _____

4. _____ (8 words)

   _____

5. _____ (12 words)

   _____

6. _____ (9 words)

   _____

7. _____ (9 words)

   _____

8. _____ (11 words)

   _____

ACTIVITY 5 **Matching words with definitions**

Match each word with its definition.

1. _____ absolute (*adj.*)

2. _____ characteristic (*n.*)

3. _____ especially (*adv.*)

4. _____ explore (*tr.v.*)

5. _____ geographer (*n.*)

6. _____ liberty (*n.*)

7. _____ origin (*n.*)

8. _____ refer (*intr.v.*)

9. _____ variety (*n.*)

10. _____ weather (*n.*)

a. Freedom from imprisonment, slavery, or forced labor.

b. Just for a special purpose; to a very great degree, uncommonly.

c. Different types of things.

d. A feature or quality that identifies or distinguishes sthg. or sbdy.

e. To investigate sthg. systematically; examine.

f. The source or beginning of sthg; root.

g. Without comparison with other objects; actual; real.

h. A person who studies geography: the earth and its features, including human life and the effects of human activity.

i. A portion of land nearly surrounded by water, but connected to the mainland.

j. Temperature, moisture, wind, air pressure, and other conditions of the atmosphere.

k. To be about; concern.

ACTIVITY 6 **Learning the academic vocabulary**

Look up each academic word in an English dictionary. Copy the pronunciation of each word exactly. Use the part of speech to guide you to the right entry. Write the syllable-stress code. Study the definition. Then compare your answers with a classmate's. The first one is done for you.

1. area
(*n.*)   _____ar•e•a_____   _____âr´ē-ə_____   [__3__ - __1__]
A distinct part or section of land.

2. aspect
(*n.*)   _____   _____   [___ - ___]
A feature, or part of a whole.

3. constantly
(*adv.*)   _____   _____   [___ - ___]
Again and again without end; continually occurring.

4. coordinate
(*n.*)   _____   _____   [___ - ___]
Each of a set of numbers that describe the exact position of sthg. such as a place on a map.

5. diversity
(*n.*)   _____   _____   [___ - ___]
Variety; the fact or quality of being diverse or different.

6. environment
(*n.*)   _____   _____   [___ - ___]
All of the surroundings and conditions that affect the growth and development of living things.

7. factor
(*n.*)   _____   _____   [___ - ___]
Sthg. that causes a certain result; an element or ingredient.

8. feature
(*n.*)   _____   _____   [___ - ___]
An important part of something that makes it different from other things.

9. interact
(*intr.v.*)   _____   _____   [___ - ___]
To have an effect on each other; to be involved in communication or social activity with each other.

10. location   ——————————   ——————————   [—— - ——]
    (*n.*)
             The place or position of sthg., a place where sthg.
             is located.

11. natural resources   ——————————   ——————————   [—— - ——]
    (*n. phr.*)
             Raw materials found in nature, such as minerals,
             trees, fresh water, and oil, that are necessary or
             useful to humans.

12. region   ——————————   ——————————   [—— - ——]
    (*n.*)
             A large portion of the earth's surface.

13. revolution   ——————————   ——————————   [—— - ——]
    (*n.*)
             The overthrow of one government and its
             replacement with another.

14. theme   ——————————   ——————————   [—— - ——]
    (*n.*)
             A central idea or main pattern, such as in daily life
             or an artistic work.

15. traffic   ——————————   ——————————   [—— - ——]
    (*n.*)
             The movement of cars and trucks along the road in
             a particular area.

ACTIVITY 7   **Checking and pronouncing the academic words**

Listen to the pronunciation of each word in the previous activity. Check the
syllable-stress code. Pronounce each word with your instructor or the
recording, and then practice with a partner.

ACTIVITY 8   Listening to the academic words in context

Listen to the sentences and complete each one with a selection from the academic word list in Activity 6. Sometimes you will hear different forms of the words on the list. Write the form that you hear.

1. The physical and cultural _____ of the United States is impressive.

2. Physical geography involves all the natural _____ on the earth.

3. One of the _____ of geography is location.

4. The _____ between humans and the environment is another theme of geography.

5. Physical and human _____ both affect place.

6. People interact with their _____ in many ways.

7. People _____ move in search of better places to live.

8. _____ jams are one negative result of human-environment interaction.

9. The United States varies greatly in its physical features, _____ _____, climates, and people.

10. A _____ may be as large as a continent, or as small as a neighborhood.

11. The _____ of latitude and longitude give the absolute _____ of a place.

12. The United States ranks third in both total _____ and population in the world.

13. If you can recognize and understand the five major themes, you will understand all the different _____ of geography.

ACTIVITY 9 **Listening to numbers in context**

In Chapter 2, you practiced listening to numbers and exchanging information with number phrases.[1] Now you will hear number phrases in the context of the geography of the United States.

Listen to the sentences and write the numbers you hear.

1. The United States covers —————————— square miles.

2. Mount McKinley in Alaska reaches —————————— feet above sea level.

3. In contrast, Death Valley in California is very low at —————————— feet below sea level.

4. Plains make up almost —————————— of the country.

5. Mountains and plateaus each make up —————————— of the country.

6. In Alaska, —————————— lakes dot the landscape.

7. —————————— percent of the United States is farmed, and this amount provides the country with a steady food supply.

8. Urban areas cover only about —————————— percent of the nation.

9. The United States contains a variety of climates. For example, the average temperature in January in Miami, Florida, is —————————— degrees Fahrenheit, while it is —————————— degrees Fahrenheit in Minneapolis, Minnesota.

10. Between —————————— and —————————— species and subspecies of plants and vegetation grow in the United States.

11. This includes over —————————— different kinds of trees.

1. Review Chapter 2 Activities 9, 10, 11, 21, 22, 23, 24, 26.

Getting Information from the Lecture

STRATEGY

Listening for Details

The lecturer for this chapter begins with an introduction about geography. He states that a very useful way to think about geography is in terms of major themes. He tells us the number of major themes. This prepares us to listen for details of these major themes in the main body of the lecture.

You'll recall that some lecturers use questions to make listeners focus on the answers. Sometimes this lecturer asks questions, just like the one in Chapter 2, *Nutrition and Human Health*. A question may mark an important point, so remember to use this to help you understand.

You will listen to the lecture several times. Each time you will listen for a specific purpose.

 ACTIVITY 10 Getting a preview: Lecture Part 1

Your instructor will play the lecture for you. Listen to the introduction and choose the best answer to complete each sentence. You may listen more than once.

1. The lecturer welcomes students to a ——— geography class.
   a. cultural
   b. physical
   c. both a and b
2. The lecturer says that the best place to begin the study of American history is with ———.
   a. its geography
   b. a course syllabus
   c. neither
3. ——— means *earth*.
   a. Geo
   b. Graph or graphy
   c. Description

4. Geography is the study of ——.
   a. land
   b. water
   c. people
   d. environment
   e. all of the above

5. The United States is part of ——.
   a. America
   b. the North American country
   c. the North American continent

6. The United States has an enormous variety of ——.
   a. physical features
   b. natural resources
   c. climates
   d. people
   e. all of the above

7. If you can recognize and understand —— important themes, you will understand all the different aspects of geography.
   a. three
   b. four
   c. five
   d. six
   e. seven

8. The lecture is probably given ——.
   a. on the first day of the course
   b. on the day before a midterm exam

9. How many times did you need to listen to complete the sentences above?
   a. 1
   b. 2
   c. 3 or more

ACTIVITY 11 **Listening for major points: Lecture Part 2**

After the introduction, the lecturer begins to present new information. He explains all of the themes of geography. Using Boston, he gives examples to help us understand each theme. When you listen for the first time, focus on hearing the major themes.

Take out five coins (e.g., pennies) and put them on your desk. Your instructor will play the lecture for you. Whenever you hear one of the major themes, put a coin in your hand. Your instructor may stop the lecture and ask you to say what the theme is. Get ready!

After you have collected five coins, you are rich with information!

Master Student Tip

▼ Listen for number phrases that enumerate main ideas, like *the five major themes* or *the second reason.* Also listen for phrases that include words like *major, main, important*, and *necessary.* This will help you identify the significant points of a lecture. Take note of these important points to use when you prepare for tests and other assignments.

ACTIVITY 12 Focusing on transition words: Parts 1 and 2

Many lecturers use transition words to enumerate, *or list, things one by one. They may give the listeners a preview by saying the total number of items or kinds. When you hear sentences like the ones below, you should listen for more information about each item or kind. Count each one as you listen.*

Today we'll examine the five major themes of geography.

I'm going to show you the two main ways to save your files.

There are four important reasons that you should review for the exam.

In spoken English, the -s and -es endings are pronounced in three different ways.

Let's look at several factors that affect the geography of the northeast region.

Many kinds of people at the college help students reach their educational goals.

Sometimes a lecturer doesn't tell you the total number at the beginning. You hear the first item or kind, and then you hear more. When you hear a phrase that includes "one (kind)" or "the first (kind)," you should be ready to listen for "another (kind)," "the second (kind)," or "the next (kind)."

The first purpose of this activity . . . The second purpose . . .
The third one . . .
One special characteristic of this architecture . . .
Another characteristic . . .
The most common kind of bird . . . Another common kind . . .
The first necessary step . . . The next thing to do . . .
The last thing to do . . .

Listen to this part of the lecture again on the (student) website at http://esl.college.hmco.com/students. As you listen, write the transitions you hear. You may listen more than once. The first one is done for you.

1. A very useful way to think about geography is in terms of
   major themes , uh, _major ideas,_ , or _themes_ .

2. In this class, we're going to examine the _____
   _____ _____ of geography: location,
   place, region, movement, and human-environment interaction.

3. If you can recognize—recognize and understand—

_____ _____ _____ ,

you will understand all the different aspects of geography.

4. Now, don't worry if you don't understand _____

_____ _____ yet, all right?

5. Let me explain how _____ _____

_____ apply to Boston.

6. So, the question "Where is Boston" is about its location. Now that's

_____ _____ _____ of

geography. What's _____ _____

_____ ? Right, location.

7. Moving on to _____ _____

_____ , let's ask the question "What is Boston like?" To

describe Boston, place, _____ _____

_____ of geography, can help you answer this question.

8. What about region? This is _____

_____ _____ _____ .

9. _____ _____ _____ of

geography is movement.

10. Human-environment interaction is _____

_____ _____ . This

_____ _____ refers to ways people interact

with their environment.

11. This semester, we'll explore _____

_____ _____ _____

_____ in America: location, place, region, movement,

and human-environment interaction.

ACTIVITY 13 Focusing on examples: Lecture Part 2

 **STRATEGY**

Listening for Examples

Many lecturers give examples to support their major ideas. Some examples are general, and others are specific. In this lecture, the lecturer gives general examples about each theme of geography. He also gives specific examples of how each theme applies to Boston.

Listen to this part of the lecture again. Listen for both general and specific examples. In the outline that follows, underline one of the words in the parentheses or fill in each blank with a word or phrase. You may listen more than once. The first one is done for you.

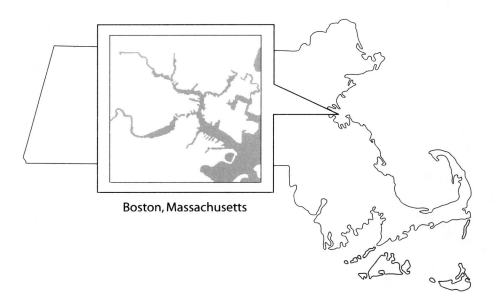

Boston, Massachusetts

Themes of Geography

I. Location

* General: (two / three) kinds of location:
    * Relative location (decides / describes) where a certain area is in (reference / relation) to another area.
    * Absolute location uses the (coordinates / characteristics) of (altitude / latitude) and (longitude / liberty)
* Specific: Boston
    * relative location: (northeast / southeast) corner of the United States next to the (Atlantic / Pacific) Ocean
    * absolute location: (24° / 42°) north latitude and 71° (west / east) longitude.

II. _____

* General: Place (refers / prefers) to two factors that make one area (difficult / different) from another.
    * (Physical / Essential) factors: natural (features / reasons), such as physical setting, (planets / plants), animals, and (weather / water).
    * (Individual / Human) factors include (constant / cultural) diversity.
* Specific: Boston
    * Physical factors: a hilly (peninsula / island) surrounded by (natural resources / water)
    * Human factors: (Arab / African) American, Irish, Italian, (Chinese / Japanese) and (Hispanic / French)

III. _____

* General: (Geographers / Geologists) break the (word / world) into regions as (lot / large) as a continent, or as small as a (neighbor / neighborhood).
    * A (origin / region) has shared (characteristics / variety): Political division, (structure / climate), (language / revolution), religion
* Specific: Boston
    * Boston, (New York / Chicago), and Philadelphia are part of the (southwest / northeast) region. These cities share a (climate / government)

IV. _____

- General: Movement of (people / animals) goods, and (weather / ideas) from one place to another
  - Specific: Boston
    - Concepts of (diversity / freedom) and self-government (developed / explored) in Boston and (spread / referred) to the other colonies. That (traffic / movement) led to the formation of the (dependent / independent) United States.

V. Human-_____ interaction

- General: Building a (region / road), cutting down a (tree / street), or even (sitting / seating) in the sun.
- Specific: Boston
  - (six miles / sixty meters) of green parkland in Boston called the Emerald (Necklace / Belt)

📄 Using your Notes to Answer Questions

🎧 **ACTIVITY 14 Comprehending the lecture**

You will hear ten statements about the lecture. Refer to your notes in Activities 10–13 and your auditory memory. After listening to each statement, circle True or False according to your information.

1. True   False

2. True   False

3. True   False

4. True   False

5. True   False

6. True   False

7. True   False

8. True   False

9. True   False

10. True   False

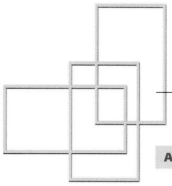

Part 2

ACTIVITY 15 Retelling the content of the lecture

STRATEGY

Retelling to Check Comprehension

Retelling helps you check your comprehension. It helps you prepare for class discussions. It helps you prepare for a test. Classmates help each other by retelling the lecture.

Work in pairs to retell the information in the lecture. Look at the notes you wrote in Activities 10–13, where you focused on major ideas, transitions, and examples. You do not need to remember the lecturer's exact words, but you must remember the ideas. You may paraphrase these ideas. Your instructor may ask you to retell the whole lecture at once or to practice retelling it in two parts:

> Part 1: The introduction (the first three minutes of the lecture)
> Part 2: The body (the last seven minutes of the lecture)

Lecture: First Retelling

> **Speaker:** Retell the lecture to your partner. Use your notes to remind you of the content.
>
> **Listener:** Remind the speaker of missing points by giving some keywords or ideas. Ask questions for clarification.
>
> Take turns.

Lecture: Second Retelling

> **Speaker:** Retell the lecture to your partner. This time, however, do not use your notes. Look at your listener.
>
> **Listener:** Remind the speaker of missing points by giving some keywords or ideas. Confirm orally what you hear.
>
> Take turns. Your instructor may call on you to retell some of the information in the lecture to the whole class.

ACTIVITY **16**   **Checking how well you retold the lecture**

Answer the questions about yourself. Then discuss your answers with a partner.

1. Which parts of the lecture were easy for you to retell? Put a plus (+) beside the easy parts. Put a minus (−) beside the difficult parts. Tell why you found them easy or difficult.

    _____ The introduction: General information about geography

    _____ The theme of Location

    _____ The theme of Place

    _____ The theme of Region

    _____ The theme of Movement

    _____ The theme of Human-Environment interaction

2. Which kind of information was easier for you to retell? Put a plus (+) by the easy parts. Put a minus (−) by the difficult parts. Tell why you found them easy or difficult.

    _____ The general ideas

    _____ The examples

3. In what ways did you and your partner help each other retell the information accurately? Put a check by all the statements that are true.

    _____ I told my partner the missing or incorrect information that I read in my notes.

    _____ I told my partner the missing or incorrect information that I recalled from my memory.

    _____ I gave my partner hints about the missing or incorrect information that I read in my notes.

    _____ I gave my partner hints about the missing or incorrect information that I recalled from my memory.

    _____ I asked my partner questions about the missing or incorrect information.

    _____ My partner retold everything perfectly. I did not need to help my partner.

    _____ I retold everything perfectly. My partner did not need to help me.

ACTIVITY 17 Learning compass directions

> *East* is the direction that lies directly ahead of you as you face the rising sun. When you face east, *west* is behind you. *North* is to your left. *South* is to your right. North, south, east, and west are the four cardinal points of the compass. On most maps of the world, north is shown at the top of the page.

Label the directions on the compass rose. Use these abbreviations:

North = N

South = S

East = E

West = W

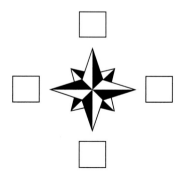

Stand up. Your instructor will call out the four cardinal directions, one at a time. Face that direction. Then practice with a partner.

Listen to the pronunciation of the noun and adjective forms of the directions. Then answer the questions that follow.

Noun	Adjective
east	eastern
west	western
north	northern
south	southern
northeast	northeastern
northwest	northwestern
southeast	southeastern
southwest	southwestern
center	central

1. What suffix is added to most directions to make them adjectives?

   _____

2. How does the word *center* change to become an adjective?

   _____

Notice the difference between the th sounds in north-northern, and south-southern.

3. In which words is the th sound voiceless?

   _____

4. In which words is the th sound voiced?

   _____

Notice the difference in vowel sounds in south (south) and southern (sŭth′ ə rn).

5. Which word has the vowel sound as in *cow*?

   _____

6. Which word has the vowel sound as in *cup*?

   _____

ACTIVITY 18   **Learning the abbreviations of the states**

> Each of the fifty states and the District of Columbia has a two-letter abbreviation. These short forms are used on small maps and for mailing letters.

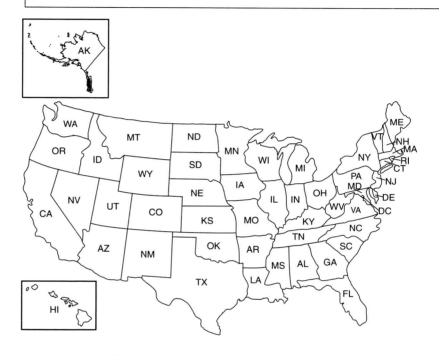

Listen to the abbreviations and the names of the states.

AL	Alabama	ID	Idaho	MT	Montana	RI	Rhode Island
AK	Alaska	IL	Illinois	NE	Nebraska	SC	South Carolina
AZ	Arizona	IN	Indiana	NV	Nevada	SD	South Dakota
AR	Arkansas	IA	Iowa	NH	New	TN	Tennessee
CA	California	KS	Kansas		Hampshire	TX	Texas
CO	Colorado	KY	Kentucky	NJ	New Jersey	UT	Utah
CT	Connecticut	LA	Louisiana	NM	New Mexico	VT	Vermont
DE	Delaware	ME	Maine	NY	New York	VA	Virginia
DC	Washington,	MD	Maryland	NC	North Carolina	WA	Washington
	District of	MA	Massachusetts	ND	North Dakota	WV	West Virginia
	Columbia	MI	Michigan	OH	Ohio	WI	Wisconsin
FL	Florida	MN	Minnesota	OK	Oklahoma	WY	Wyoming
GA	Georgia	MS	Mississippi	OR	Oregon		
HI	Hawaii	MO	Missouri	PA	Pennsylvania		

POWER GRAMMAR

Phrases of Relative Location and Direction

The directions, such as *north, east, southeast,* and *northwest,* can mean the part of an area, region, or country that is located in or toward that direction.[2] They are nouns in the following sentences:

> The Midwest includes the states of Kansas and Ohio.
> The South includes Texas and Missouri.
> The Northwest includes Oregon and Idaho.

To show location within an area, use the preposition *in*:
prep + (art) + (adj) + noun.

> Massachusetts is located in the northeast.
> Missouri is in the central part of the country.
> Do your friends live in eastern Michigan?

To show movement *to, from,* or *around* a place, use prepositional phrases such as these:

> We're going to the Midwest next May.
> Our neighbors moved here from the east.
> They toured around the southeastern states last summer.

To show that Place A is located *outside of* Place B, use adverb phrases:

> Utah is located east of Nevada.
> Wyoming is north of Colorado.
> Miami is far south of New York City.

---

2. When they refer to a region, they may be capitalized, e.g., *the North, the East,* and *the Midwest.*

ACTIVITY 19 **Placing stress on choice questions**

> A choice question contains the word *or* and allows you to choose between two things. We usually stress the topic and the choices. We use rising intonation on the first choice and falling intonation on the second choice.

Listen to the examples. Underline the topic and choices. Draw a rising arrow over the first choice and a falling arrow over the second choice. The first one is done for you.

1. Is <u>Boston</u> in the <u>east</u> or the <u>west</u>?

2. Is Montana in the north or the south?

3. Is California on the Atlantic Ocean or the Pacific Ocean?

4. Are there mountains in Colorado or Kansas?

5. Is Ohio east or west of Indiana?

6. Is Hawaii an island or a peninsula?

7. Which state is a peninsula: Georgia or Florida?

8. Which state is bigger: Texas or Oklahoma?

9. Which state is south of Missouri: Iowa or Arkansas?

10. Where is Massachusetts: north of Vermont or south of Vermont?

Practice in pairs. Ask the choice questions above. Stress the topic and the choices. Use rising intonation on the first choice and falling intonation on the second choice. Using the maps on pages 77 and 99, answer the questions in complete sentences.

ACTIVITY 20 Listening to dialogues about place

Look at the maps and listen to the dialogues. Listen for phrases of relative location and direction. Write the phrases in the blanks.

Dialogue 1

A: Is Utah _____ or _____ _____
Colorado?

B: Neither. Utah is _____ _____ Colorado.
Look at the map.

A: Oh, I see. Wyoming is _____ _____
Colorado.

B: New Mexico is _____ _____ Colorado.

A: And Kansas is _____ _____ Colorado.

B: That's right.

Dialogue 2

A: How many states have the name _____ in them?

B: Let's see . . . there's _____ Dakota. And of course
_____ _____ it is _____
Dakota. They're both in _____ _____
_____ _____ the U.S.A.

A: Uh-huh. Name another one.

B: _____ Carolina.

A: _____ and _____ Carolina are on
_____ _____ seaboard, aren't they?

B: Yes, they are right on the Atlantic Ocean. But they're not
considered to be in _____ _____
_____ .

Dialogue 3

A: Which state is in ———————— far ————————?

B: Alaska. It's ———————— ———————— Canada, and

Canada is ———————— ———————— the United States.

A: Which state is in ———————— ————————

————————?

B: The ————————? Maine. Its nickname is the Pine Tree State.

A: Which state is in ———————— far ————————?

B: Florida, the Sunshine State.

A: Where's Hawaii?

B: Hawaii is far ———————— ———————— the mainland,

in the Pacific Ocean. It's called the Aloha State.

Dialogue 4

A: Texas is ———————— ———————— ————————,

isn't it?

B: Yes, right on the border of Mexico.

A: Is Georgia ———————— ———————— ————————?

B: It sure is.

A: How about New Jersey?

B: That's ———————— ———————— ————————.

A: And Oregon?

B: Oregon is ———————— ———————— ————————.

Dialogue 5

A: Is Sunnyvale in ———————— or ———————— California?

B: Sunnyvale's in ———————— California. It's not far from

San Francisco.

A: How about Los Angeles?

B: L.A.? It's in ───────── California.

A: Where's Fresno?

B: Fresno's in ───────── California.

Practice the dialogues with a partner. Use proper stress and intonation for questions and statements.

ACTIVITY 21 Asking about the location of the states

Work with a partner. Using the map of the United States, ask and answer questions about the location of various states. Refer to Power Grammar: Phrases of Relative Location and Direction. Use the dialogues in Activity 20 as models.

ACTIVITY 22 Listening to U.S. city names

> Some city names are one word. Others are composed of two or more words, but they are pronounced together as one.

Master Student Tip

Listen for language patterns in vocabulary, grammar, and pronunciation. Use these patterns when you speak. Other people will understand you better.

Listen to the names of some cities in the United States. Write the syllable-stress code. The first one is done for you.

1. Baltimore   [_3_ ˉ _⌄_]   9. Los Angeles[3]   [___ - ___]
2. Boston   [___ - ___]   10. Madison   [___ - ___]
3. Chicago   [___ - ___]   11. Miami   [___ - ___]
4. Cincinnati   [___ - ___]   12. Montgomery   [___ - ___]
5. Detroit   [___ - ___]   13. Philadelphia   [___ - ___]
6. Honolulu   [___ - ___]   14. Salt Lake City   [___ - ___]
7. Houston   [___ - ___]   15. San Francisco   [___ - ___]
8. Juneau   [___ - ___]   16. Washington, D.C. [___ - ___]

Pronounce the names of the cities above. Pay attention to the syllables and stress.

Write the names of six cities in your local area. Mark the syllable-stress code for each one. Pronounce the names of the cities to a partner.

_____ [___ - ___]   _____ [___ - ___]

_____ [___ - ___]   _____ [___ - ___]

_____ [___ - ___]   _____ [___ - ___]

3. Its short name, L.A., sounds like "Ellay." [2 - 2].

ACTIVITY 23 **Learning about latitude and longitude**

Latitude is an imaginary line that runs east to west around the earth. Latitude lines are all of equal distance north or south of the equator. Latitude lines show distance in degrees north or south of the equator. The equator is a latitude line that circles the earth halfway between the North and South Poles. It measures 0° latitude.

Longitude is an imaginary line that runs north to south around the earth. Longitude lines are closer together near the North and South Poles and farther apart near the equator. The Prime Meridian is a longitude line that runs from the North Pole to the South Pole passing through Greenwich, England. It measures 0° longitude.

Latitude and longitude lines appear together on a map. These lines allow you to pinpoint[4] the absolute location of cities and other geographic features. For example, the city of Boston, Massachusetts, lies at approximately 42 degrees north latitude and 71 degrees west longitude, or 42° N 71° W.

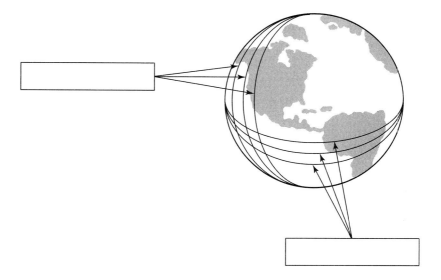

Look at the picture of the earth. Write either the word latitude *or* longitude *in the correct box.*

4. *pinpoint* (*tr.v.*) = to identify or locate sthg. accurately

ACTIVITY 24 **Learning about the Global Positioning System**

The Global Positioning System, or GPS, measures latitude and longitude. It gives absolute location. GPS was originally made for military purposes. Now there are many everyday uses, too. If you are hiking in the woods or driving a car on the road, understanding latitude and longitude can be helpful. You can identify your location. Some cell phones have a GPS receiver inside. If you dial 911, emergency services know exactly where to find you.

Discuss and put a check (✓) beside the people who may find latitude and longitude useful for their occupations.

_____ actors	_____ pilots
_____ astronauts	_____ police officers
_____ bakers	_____ sailors
_____ emergency medical workers	_____ soccer players
_____ farmers	_____ soldiers
_____ firefighters	_____ tailors
_____ hikers	_____ taxi drivers
_____ mapmakers	_____ travelers
_____ oceangraphers	_____ tunnel construction workers

ACTIVITY 25 Identifying cities by absolute location

The dotted lines on this map of the United States indicate latitude and longitude. The degrees of latitude are shown on the left, and the degrees of longitude are shown at the top. The four black dots indicate cities.

Listen to the sentences telling the absolute location of cities in the United States. Write the names of the cities in the boxes. Afterward, check your answers with the class.

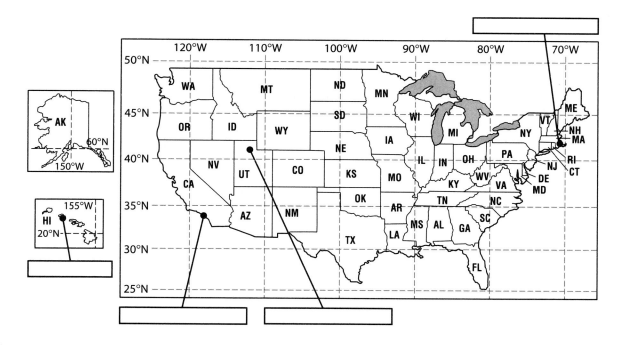

ACTIVITY 26   **Placing the cities on the map**

In this activity, you will exchange information orally about the location of cities in the United States. You will use degrees of latitude and longitude. On the map, you will see sixteen dots. Each dot represents a city. The map shows the names of ten cities, but the names of six cities are missing. Your partner's map shows the names of ten cities, but the names of six different cities are missing. By speaking and listening, you will both be able to fill in the names of all of the cities. Use the previous activity as a model. Ask for confirmation and clarification.

Work in pairs. Decide who is Partner A and who is Partner B.
Take turns. When it is your turn to speak, read one sentence to your partner. When it is your turn to listen, check and confirm meaning. Ask for repetition, repeat the speaker's exact words, and ask about spelling. Refer to Chapter 1, Activity 18 Asking for clarification, page 20, and Chapter 2, Activity 20 Asking for confirmation and clarification, page 57.

For example:

Excuse me. What is the latitude of that city?
Please repeat the longitude.
Did you say at 34 degrees north latitude and 118 degrees west longitude, I will find Los Angeles?
How do you spell Los Angeles?

After confirming the information, write down the name of the city on the correct place on your map. Take turns listening and speaking. After filling in all of the missing cities, compare your answers with your partner's. Do NOT look at your partner's page until both of you finish the activity.

Partner A, turn to page 112. Partner B, turn to Appendix page 260.

ACTIVITY 27 Checking your communication strategies

Answer the questions after completing Activity 26.

1. As a speaker, did you pronounce the names of cities and other words (e.g., *located, degrees, north, latitude, longitude*) with the correct number of syllables and proper stress?

   none   a few   some   many

2. As a listener, did you check and confirm your partner's information by asking questions about location and spelling?

   none   a few   some   many

3. As a speaker, which information was the easiest for you to <u>say</u> to your partner?

   _____

   _____

4. As a listener, which information was the easiest for you to <u>understand</u> from your partner?

   _____

   _____

5. Do you need to improve any listening or speaking skill mentioned above? If so, which one(s)?

   _____

   _____

For Activity 26 Partner A
Partner B, turn to page 262.

You and your partner have different information. When you speak, pronounce clearly. When you listen, check and confirm your understanding. Fill in the name of the city on your map.

1. Baltimore is located at 39 degrees north latitude and 77 degrees west longitude.
2. Miami is located at 26 degrees north latitude and 80 degrees west longitude.
3. Houston is located at 30 degrees north latitude and 95 degrees west longitude.
4. Juneau is located at 58 degrees north latitude and 135 degrees west longitude.
5. At 43 degrees north latitude and 89 degrees west longitude, you will find Madison.
6. At 42 degrees north latitude and 83 degrees west longitude, you will find Detroit.

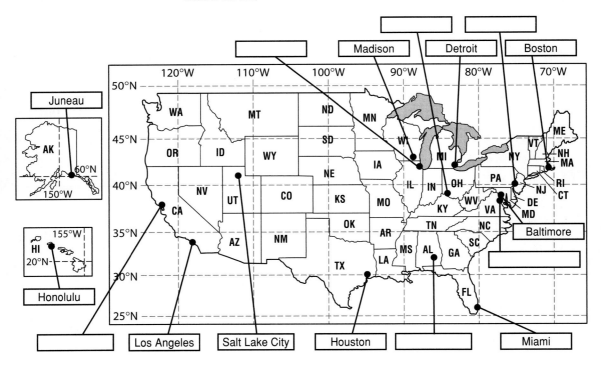

After filling in all the missing cities, check your map with your partner. Then continue with Activity 27 on page 111.

POWER GRAMMAR

To ask about distance, we use **How far**.

How far is it to the public library?
It's about five miles from here.
How far is it from here to the next bus stop?
It's about three hundred yards.
How far is it to the art studio from here?
It's just up the stairs and to your left.

To ask about the duration of time, we use **How long**.

How long is the class?
It's 50 minutes.
How long is the semester?
It's 16 weeks long.
How long is the movie?
It's an hour and a half.

We also use this sentence pattern to ask about the duration of time: **How long** *does it take* + infinitive.

How long does it take to get from here to the childcare center?
It takes only two minutes.
How long did it take you to do the assignment?
It took me two and a half hours.
How long will it take to finish your A.A. degree?
It will take me three more semesters.

ACTIVITY 28 Determining how far and how long

Listen to the questions and answers above. Underline the stressed words.

With a partner, practice asking and answering the questions above. Use the rise-falling WH-question intonation pattern when you ask How far, How long, *and* How long does it take to. *Use this same intonation pattern when you say the answers.*

Unscramble the words on the next page to make a question. Capitalize the first word, and end the sentence with a question mark. The first one is done for you. Next, write an appropriate answer to each question. Refer to Power Grammar: Talking about Distance and Time. Finally, practice the dialogues with a partner. Pronounce the content words long and the function words short.

1. classes how is between break long the

   Q. _How long is the break between classes?_

   A. _____

2. bookstore far it how here to is the from

   Q. _____

   A. _____

3. get how to you school it take long to does

   Q. _____

   A. _____

4. the is far coffee shop to how it

   Q. _____

   A. _____

5. session the long how counseling yesterday was

   Q. _____

   A. _____

6. restroom how it nearest to far the is

   Q. _____

   A. _____

7. did long read it how you lesson to take the last

   Q. _____

   A. _____

8. how office it to instructor's is far our

   Q. _____

   A. _____

9. it will chapter long complete us this take how to

   Q. _____

   A. _____

ACTIVITY 29 Presenting information about a place

Choose one city, state, or region. Bring to class a picture, map, or postcard of this place. Prepare a short talk (four to six minutes) about the geography of that place. Choose three of the five major themes of geography to guide you. Form a group of four students. Take turns speaking and listening.

Speaker: Show your partners your picture, map, or postcard. Tell why you chose to present this place. Talk about the place in terms of three of the five major themes of geography. As you speak, remember to use proper vocabulary, grammar, and pronunciation.

Listeners: Repeat the speaker's key information to confirm your understanding. Ask questions for clarification. Take brief notes in the chart below. Use the blank spaces for additional information.

Partner's name			
Name of place			
Geography theme: Location			
Geography theme: Place			
Geography theme: Region			
Movement			
Human-Environment interaction			
Other interesting points			

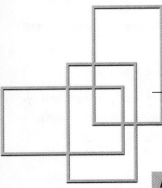

Part 3

ASSESSING YOUR LISTENING AND SPEAKING SKILLS

ACTIVITY 30 **Applying skills from the chapter**

Many of the following questions will help you review the five major themes of geography and connect the themes to the geography that you are familiar with. Some of the questions will help you review listening and speaking skills. These types of questions may be on a test.

Your instructor may ask you to write down the answers to the questions, discuss these questions in a group, and/or record your oral answers to the questions.

Prepare answers to these questions. Then discuss them with a group of three or four students.

1. LOCATION: Where is your school located? (You can answer with absolute or relative location. Refer to Power Grammar: Phrases of Relative Location and Direction, page 100).

   _____

   _____

2. LOCATION: Where is your home located? (You can answer with absolute or relative location.)

   _____

   _____

3. PLACE: What is the name of the place where you live now?

   _____

   a. Describe one or more physical features of that place. (For example, physical setting—landforms, water—plants, animals, weather. Refer to Activity 1. Basic landforms, page 78.)

   _____

   _____

    b. Describe one or more human features of that place. (For example, kind of people, language, art, architecture)

    _____

    _____

4. PLACE: Choose one place that is different from the place in #3: your place of origin or another place that you know very well. What

is the name of that place? _____

    a. Describe one or more physical features of that place. (For example, physical setting—landforms, water—plants, animals, weather)

    _____

    _____

    b. Describe one or more human features of that place. (For example, kind of people, language, art, architecture)

    _____

    _____

5. REGION: Choose two similar places that are nearby (two cities, two areas, two states, two countries). What are the names of those

places? _____ and _____

Describe two or three characteristics that these two places share with each other. (For example, political division, climate, language, or religion)

_____

_____

6. MOVEMENT: Give two examples of how you travel from one place to another.

_____

_____

7. MOVEMENT: Name two ways that you spread information and ideas.

_____

_____

8. HUMAN-ENVIRONMENT INTERACTION: Choose a place and
write its name here. _____ Name two ways (one
positive and one negative) that people in that place have affected their
environment.

_____

_____

9. HUMAN-ENVIRONMENT INTERACTION: Choose a place and
write its name here. _____ Name two ways (one
positive and one negative) that the environment has affected the
people in that place.

_____

_____

10. Which of the five themes of geography has most affected your life:
location, place, region, movement, or human-environment
interaction? (Underline it.) Please explain.

_____

_____

_____

11. If you listen for transition words that enumerate, how can this help
you focus on ideas?

_____

_____

12. When should you use how far and when should you use how long?
Explain your answer, and give two examples of each.

_____

_____

13. Draw a rising arrow ↗ or a falling arrow ↘ over the underlined words in the following sentences. Why should you pronounce it with that intonation?

   a. San Francisco is in the <u>west</u>. _____

   b. Is San Francisco in the <u>east</u>? _____

   c. Is San Francisco in the <u>west</u> or the <u>east</u>? _____

   d. Where is San <u>Francisco</u>? _____

ACTIVITY 31   Focusing on transition words that enumerate

Listen again to the lecture in Chapter 1, The Power of Music. *Listen for eight transition phrases that enumerate major points. You will hear one of the three in each of the eight items below. Underline the one transition phrase that you hear.*

1.	a. one power	b. one way	c. first
2.	a. two kinds	b. secondly	c. a second power
3.	a. thirdly	b. three important reasons	c. a third power
4.	a. another power	b. another reason	c. other ways
5.	a. four important reasons	b. the fourth thing	c. a fourth power
6.	a. five types	b. a fifth power	c. the fifth connection
7.	a. the last power	b. lastly	c. at last
8.	a. the sixth way	b. sixthly	c. six different ways

ACTIVITY 32   **Reviewing pronunciation, stress, and fluency**

Review these words and dialogues. Write the syllable-stress code for words 1–15. Draw the intonation lines over the keywords in dialogues 16–18. Then practice with a partner. Pronounce each item as clearly as you can. Have your partner listen and help you with your pronunciation of syllables and stress. Take turns. Your instructor may ask you to record your pronunciation of these items and others in this chapter.

1. major	[___ - ___]	**9.** southern	[___ - ___]
2. theme	[___ - ___]	**10.** northwestern	[___ - ___]
3. environment	[___ - ___]	**11.** Philadelphia	[___ - ___]
4. variety	[___ - ___]	**12.** Chicago	[___ - ___]
5. geography	[___ - ___]	**13.** Los Angeles	[___ - ___]
6. area	[___ - ___]	**14.** Washington, D.C.	[___ - ___]
7. origin	[___ - ___]	**15.** Miami	[___ - ___]
8. central	[___ - ___]		

16. A: How high is Mount McKinley in Alaska?

   B: Very high. It reaches 20,320 feet above sea level.

17. A: How far is it from Miami to New York City?

   B: It's 1,088 miles from Miami to New York, as the crow flies.[5]

18. A: How long does it take you to drive to school?

   B: It takes me from twenty to thirty-five minutes, depending on the traffic.

5. *as the crow flies* (idiom) = in a straight line

ACTIVITY 33   **Taking dictation**

In this dictation you will hear vocabulary and sentence patterns that you practiced in this chapter. Your instructor will tell you the number of words in each sentence. Write the numbers within the parentheses and use them as a guide. You will hear each sentence three times. First, listen and try to understand the meaning of the whole sentence. Second, listen and write. Third, listen and check.

1. _____ (___ words)

   _____

2. _____ (___ words)

   _____

3. _____ (___ words)

   _____

4. _____ (___ words)

   _____

5. _____ (___ words)

   _____

6. _____ (___ words)

   _____

7. _____ (___ words)

   _____

8. _____ (___ words)

   _____

ACTIVITY 34 Summarizing your progress

How well can you perform the following objectives?

I can . . .	Barely	Somewhat	Fairly well	Very well
Use vocabulary and expressions to discuss geography.				
Use a dictionary to learn the pronunciation of new academic words.				
Recognize transitions that identify important points in a lecture.				
Understand the relationship of a main idea and an example.				
Hear, locate, and pronounce U.S. cities with proper syllables and word stress.				
Talk about information on a map.				
Ask choice questions with proper intonation.				
Ask and answer questions about location using *east*, *west*, *north* and *south*.				
Ask questions using *How far* and *How long*.				
Relate the contents of the lecture to the geography of my local area.				
Take dictation of sentences related to geography.				

WEB POWER

You will find additional exercises related to the content in this chapter at http://esl.college.hmco.com/students.

Are You Getting the Sleep You Need?

ACADEMIC FOCUS:
SCIENCE ▶ HUMAN BIOLOGY AND PSYCHOLOGY

Academic Listening and Speaking Objectives

In this chapter, you will continue to develop your skills as an academic listener and speaker. You will hear a lecture that an instructor gives on the topic of sleep. You will learn to pronounce academic vocabulary, and you will practice discussing topics related to sleep, psychology, and human biology. In particular, you will:

- Develop vocabulary and expressions to discuss sleep.
- Use a dictionary to learn the pronunciation of new academic words.
- Hear, identify, and pronounce key vocabulary with proper syllables and word stress.
- Learn the form, stress, and linking patterns and meanings of common phrasal verbs.
- Examine an analogy in a lecture.
- Distinguish main ideas from details.
- Ask questions using *What's the difference between A and B?* and *What does X mean?*
- Ask and answer questions about sleep and human behavior.
- Relate the contents of the lecture to personal sleep habits.
- Take dictation of sentences related to sleep and human behavior.

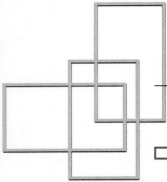

Part 1

EFFECTIVE ACADEMIC LISTENING

Getting Ready for the Lecture

Everyone sleeps, but very few people understand sleep. It is important to learn about sleep because your sleeping life affects your waking life. Knowledge about sleep is especially important for college students. In a survey of undergraduate students, the number one complaint was not getting enough sleep.[1]

ACTIVITY 1 Getting enough sleep?

Discuss the meaning of the questions and responses with your instructor. Then think about your own sleeping habits. Underline the best response to each question about yourself.

1. Do you get more or less sleep than you need?

    More than I need
    Less than I need
    Just the right amount
    I don't know

2. Do you think sleep loss is bad for you?

    Yes, it's bad
    No, it isn't bad
    I don't know

3. What is the main consequence,[2] for you, of not getting enough sleep?

    I lose energy
    I get cranky[3]
    I am less productive[4]
    Other: _____

1. Conducted by Dr. William C. Dement, Professor of Psychiatry and Behavioral Sciences at Stanford and a leading authority on sleep, sleep deprivation, and the diagnosis and treatment of sleep disorders.
2. *consequence* (*n.*) = the result of doing something
3. *cranky* (*adj.*) = easily irritated, angry and complaining
4. *productive* (*adj.*) = producing good results, useful, effective

4. How much sleep do you average on weeknights?

> Less than five hours
> Five to six hours
> Six to seven hours
> Seven to eight hours
> Eight or more hours

5. How much sleep do you average on weekends?

> Less than five hours
> Five to six hours
> Six to seven hours
> Seven to eight hours
> Eight or more hours

After you have answered the questions for yourself, form groups of four. Practice asking and answering these questions with your partners. Put a check (✓) next to all of the responses given by your partners.

 ACTIVITY 2 Learning about a national sleep survey

The Better Sleep Council[5] surveyed 1,000 adults in America about their sleep habits. The following charts show some of the results of the survey.

Listen to the sentences and fill in the missing information in the charts. Discuss the additional information to the right of each chart.

1. Do you get more or less sleep than you need?

	All	Male	Female	
More	17%	19%	___%	Men and women answered similarly, but different age groups did not. Younger people are less well-rested: 63 percent of 18 to 24-year-olds say they get less sleep than they need vs. 32 percent of those 65 and older.
Less	___%	51%	56%	
Just Right Amount	28%	___%	28%	
Don't Know	1%	2%	2%	

5. The BSC Sleep Deficit survey was conducted in January 1994 by Bruskin/Goldring Research.

2. Do you think sleep loss is bad for you?

	All	Male	Female	
Yes	___%	72%	77%	People know they should eat right and exercise regularly for good health. But they're not paying attention to the third health requirement: sleep. They know they need more sleep, but they aren't getting it.
No	21%	___%	19%	
Don't Know	4%	5%	___%	

3. What is the main consequence, for you, of not getting enough sleep?

	All	Male	Female	
Loss of Energy	48%	46%	___%	People do not have enough energy to work as hard—or play as hard—as they'd like. Why? It's due to a serious lack of sleep.
Crankiness	___%	20%	20%	
Less Productive	8%	___%	7%	
Other/ Don't Know	14%	15%	12%	

4. How much sleep do you average on weeknights?

	All	Male	Female	
Less than 5 hours	8%	___%	7%	More people suffer from a lack of sleep during the workweek.
5 to 6 hours	20%	20%	19%	
6 to 7 hours	30%	29%	___%	
7 to 8 hours	23%	22%	23%	
8 or more hours	19%	18%	20%	
Don't Know	___%	1%	3%	

5. How much sleep do you average on weekend nights?

	All	Male	Female	
Less than 5 hours	6%	5%	7%	People try to catch up on sleep on the weekends. In fact, double the number of people sleep more than eight hours on weekends as do during the week. Men are especially likely to make up lost sleep on the weekends—the percentage of men sleeping more than eight hours jumps from 18 percent to 42 percent.
5 to 6 hours	___%	9%	13%	
6 to 7 hours	21%	21%	22%	
7 to 8 hours	23%	22%	___%	
8 or more hours	38%	___%	34%	
Don't Know	1%	1%	1%	

Compare your group's results from Activity 1 with the results of the national survey above.

⬜ Looking at Language

ACTIVITY 3 Identifying syllables and stress in words

Listen to the pronunciation of these words. Clap or tap the number of syllables you hear. Then write the syllable-stress code. The first one is done for you.

1. accident (*n.*)   [_3_ - _1_]

2. alert (*n.*)   [___ - ___]

3. asleep (*n.*)   [___ - ___]

4. attention (*n.*)   [___ - ___]

5. awake (*n.*)   [___ - ___]

6. brain (*n.*)   [___ - ___]

7. conscious (*n.*)   [___ - ___]

8. conversation (*n.*)   [___ - ___]

9. debt (*n.*)   [___ - ___]

10. drowsy (*n.*)   [___ - ___]

11. recommend (*tr.v.*)   [___ - ___]

12. tendency (*n.*)   [___ - ___]

13. Which word has a silent b? _____

After you mark the syllable-stress code, take turns saying the words to your partner. Pronounce each word with the correct number of syllables. Make the stressed syllable long, strong, and high. Hear and feel the beats by clapping as you pronounce. Help your partner pronounce the words with correct syllables and stress.

ACTIVITY 4 **Taking dictation**

As you recall, taking dictation builds and assesses many language skills. Which of the following can dictation help you with?

listening	grammar	reading	vocabulary
skill	ability	comprehension	knowledge

You will hear the words from Activity 3 in context. You will hear each sentence three times. First, listen and try to understand the meaning of the whole sentence. Second, listen and write. Third, listen and check. Use the number of words in the parentheses as a guide.

1. _____ (9 words)
   _____

2. _____ (8 words)
   _____

3. _____ (10 words)
   _____

4. _____ (9 words)
   _____

5. _____ (12 words)
   _____

6. _____ (8 words)
   _____

7. _____ (12 words)
   _____

8. _____ (9 words)
   _____

ACTIVITY 5   **Matching words with definitions**

Match each word with its definition. Bonus! There is one extra definition.
Can you supply the word for it?

1. _____ accident (*n.*)

2. _____ alert (*adj.*)

3. _____ asleep (*adj.*)

4. _____ attention (*n.*)

5. _____ awake (*n.*)

6. _____ brain (*n.*)

7. _____ conscious (*adj.*)

8. _____ conversation (*n.*)

9. _____ debt (*n.*)

10. _____ drowsy (*n.*)

11. _____ recommend (*n.*)

12. _____ tendency (*n.*)

13. _____

a. Sleeping; in a state of sleep.

b. Something that is owed by a person, such as money, goods, or services.

c. To advise; to suggest (sthg. or sbdy.) to another person.

d. The organ in the head that controls all the activities of the body.

e. Something harmful or unpleasant that happens unexpectedly.

f. A talk; an informal spoken exchange of thoughts, opinions, and feelings.

g. Not asleep.

h. Producing good results, useful, effective.

i. Looking and listening carefully; concentration of the mind on sthg. or sbdy.

j. Aware of one's own environment, thoughts, and feelings.

k. Ready to act or speak; clear-headed and responsive.

l. An inclination or leaning to think, act, or behave in a certain way.

m. Dull with sleepiness.

POWER GRAMMAR

Phrasal Verbs

A phrasal verb is a short phrase made up of two or more words. The first word is a verb; the second is a particle: *go on, fall asleep.* Some phrasal verbs are made up of three words: *catch up on.* A phrasal verb has a special meaning different from the words it is made of. For example, *hand in homework* means to *submit homework.* Phrasal verbs are also called "two-word verbs" and "three-word verbs."

Many phrasal verbs have a one-word synonym.[6] The one-word synonyms are more common in formal written English. Phrasal verbs are very common in spoken English. College professors often use phrasal verbs in their lectures as they explain academic content in everyday language.

Separable and Inseparable

There are two types of phrasal verbs: separable and inseparable.
The words of a separable phrasal verb can be separated by the object.

> Correct: I <u>jotted down</u> the main idea.

> Correct: I <u>jotted</u> the main idea <u>down</u>.

When the object is a pronoun, the phrasal verb is always separated.

> Correct: I <u>jotted</u> it <u>down</u>.

> Incorrect: I <u>jotted down</u> it.

The words of an inseparable phrasal verb cannot be separated. They must always stay together.

> Correct: We <u>talked about</u> sleep.

> Correct: We <u>talked about</u> it.

> Incorrect: We <u>talked</u> sleep <u>about</u>.

> Incorrect: We <u>talked</u> it <u>about</u>.

---

6. *synonym* (*n.*) = a word that means the same as another word.

ACTIVITY 6 **Listening for phrasal verbs**

Complete the sentences with the correct form of each phrasal verb. Notice the position of the noun and pronoun objects. The first one is done for you.

Listen to the sentences and check your work. Pronounce each sentence clearly with good stress and intonation. Then practice saying them to a partner. Later, you will hear these phrasal verbs in the lecture.

Separable phrasal verbs

1. **cut out** sthg. = to remove completely, stop doing sthg.

   He'll _cut out_ coffee from his diet.

   He'll _____ coffee _____ of his diet.

   He'll _____ it _____ of his diet.

2. **find out** sthg. = to discover

   They _____ _____ her address.

   They _____ her address _____.

   They _____ it _____.

3. **hand in** sthg. = to submit

   Did you _____ _____ your homework?

   Did you _____ your homework _____?

   Did you _____ it _____?

4. **mess up** sthg. = to upset, spoil, make disorderly

   Don't _____ _____ the things on my desk.

   Don't _____ the things on my desk _____.

   Don't _____ them _____.

5. **pay back** sthg./sbdy. = to repay (a loan, a favor, etc.)

   I'll _____ _____ my debt as soon as I can.

   I'll _____ my debt _____ as soon as I can.

   I'll _____ it _____ as soon as I can.

6. **shut down** sthg. = to stop activity, close completely

They'll _____ _____ the electricity at ten.

They'll _____ the electricity _____ at ten.

They'll _____ it _____ at ten.

7. **take away** = to remove, withdraw

The bank can _____ _____ your house.

The bank can _____ your house _____.

The bank can _____ it _____.

8. **wake up** sbdy. = to awaken

Should you _____ _____ the children now?

Should you _____ the children _____ now?

Should you _____ them _____ now?

Inseparable phrasal verbs

9. **be with** = to follow, understand

Here are the directions. _____ you _____ me?

Yes, I _____ _____ you.

10. **catch up on** sthg. = to recover, complete

I must _____ _____ _____ my sleep.

I must _____ _____ _____ it tonight.

11. **cut down on** sthg. = to reduce, decrease

_____ _____ _____ caffeine and other stimulants.

_____ _____ _____ them.

12. **deal with** sthg./sbdy. = to handle, manage

Try to _____ _____ your worries before bedtime.

Try to _____ _____ them before bedtime.

13. **fall asleep** = to pass into a state or condition of sleep

    Drowsy drivers often _____ _____ at the wheel.

14. **go away** = to leave, disappear

    The pain will _____ _____ shortly.

15. **go into** = to examine, look at in detail

    We won't _____ _____ all of the reasons now.

16. **go on** = to happen

    What is _____ _____ here?

17. **go over** sthg. = to review

    Let's _____ _____ the main points.

    Let's _____ _____ them.

18. **get up** = to rise, get out of bed

    I _____ _____ at 6:00 this morning.

19. **lie down** = to recline, rest in a horizontal position

    He is going to _____ _____ on the couch.

20. **nod off** = to let the head fall forward and fall asleep

    Do you ever _____ _____ during class?

21. **stay up** = to remain awake

    She plans to _____ _____ all night to study.

22. **talk about** sthg./sbdy. = to discuss

    Let's _____ _____ the need for rest.

ACTIVITY 7 **Learning the vocabulary of academic lectures**

Look up each academic word in an English dictionary. Copy the pronunciation of each word exactly. Use the part of speech to guide you to the right entry. Write the syllable-stress code. Study the definition. Then compare your answers with a classmate's. The first one is done for you.

1. authority
   (*n.*)   <u>au•thor•i•ty</u>   <u>ə-thôr´ĭ-tē</u>   [<u>4</u> - <u>2</u>]

   Someone who is an accepted source of reliable information or advice on a subject.

2. accumulate
   (*intr. v.*)   _____   _____   [___ - ___]

   To grow or increase in number over a period of time.

3. concentrate
   (*intr. v.*)   _____   _____   [___ - ___]

   To focus all of your thoughts or mental activity on one subject or activity, usually in silence.

4. conduct
   (*tr.v.*)   _____   _____   [___ - ___]

   To manage, direct, or control something.

5. consequence
   (*n.*)   _____   _____   [___ - ___]

   A result of doing something; an effect.

6. economy
   (*n.*)   _____   _____   [___ - ___]

   The production and consumption of goods and services of a country, region, or state.

7. emphasize
   (*tr.v.*)   _____   _____   [___ - ___]

   To place importance on, to stress.

8. expert
   (*n.*)   _____   _____   [___ - ___]

   A person with a great knowledge or skill in a particular field.

9. function
   (*intr. v.*)   _____   _____   [___ - ___]

   (*n.*)   To perform (a task); to work (well, poorly, etc.). Pupose, use.

10. internal
(*adj.*)

_____ _____ [__ - __]

Inside, within, inner.

11. mechanism
(*n.*)

_____ _____ [__ - __]

A system of parts that work together to perform a particular task.

12. objective
(*adj.*)

_____ _____ [__ - __]

Factual, fair; not influenced by emotion or opinion.

13. perceive
(*tr. v.*)

_____ _____ [__ - __]

To become aware of (sbdy. or sthg.) directly through the senses (sight, hearing, touch, etc.)

14. process
(*n.*)

_____ _____ [__ - __]

Method(s) of doing something; a series of actions that make a change.

15. research
(*n.*)

_____ _____ [__ - __]

A close, careful study of a certain subject, field, or problem to discover facts or principles.

16. specific
(*adj.*)

_____ _____ [__ - __]

Exact, definite, clear, particular.

17. stimulation
(*n.*)

_____ _____ [__ - __]

An action that causes energy or activity to increase in sbdy.

18. subjective
(*adj.*)

_____ _____ [__ - __]

Based on personal opinions or emotions rather than on facts.

19. task
(*n.*)

_____ _____ [__ - __]

An assignment, a job to be performed.

ACTIVITY 8   Checking and pronouncing the vocabulary

Listen to the pronunciation of each word in Activity 7. Check the syllable-stress code.

Pronounce each word with your instructor or the recording, and then practice with a partner.

ACTIVITY 9   Listening to the academic vocabulary in context

Listen to the sentences and complete each one with a word from the academic word list in Activity 7. Sometimes you will hear different forms of the words on the list. Write the form that you hear.

1. We asked several leading _____ about sleep and sleep disorders.

2. They gave us both general and _____ information about sleep.

3. Can she _____ anything around her now?

4. No. She's fast asleep. No amount of _____ can keep her awake now.

5. What do the sleep experts _____?

6. They recommend that we _____ on healthy sleep behavior.

7. Do they _____ studies on sleepiness?

8. Yes, and they measure the subjects'[7] performance on physical and mental _____.

9. What kind of data do the scientists use in their _____?

10. They use both subjective and _____ data.

11. Is the biological clock a/an _____ _____?

12. Yes, it's a brain _____ that controls when we sleep and when we stay awake.

7. *subjects* (*n.*) = people who are looked at or examined in a scientific study.

13. How do people _____ when they haven't had enough

    sleep?

14. Very poorly. The results of sleep deprivation[8] cost the American

    _____ at least $150,000,000 a year.[9]

15. What happens when sleep debt _____?

16. Some _____ of insufficient sleep are crankiness, loss

    of energy and lower productivity.

STRATEGY

Recalling Review Material

Sometimes a lecturer begins with a review of the previous class or a
textbook reading. This is a good chance for you to recall what you
studied. If the lecturer asks you about previous material, use your
written or mental notes to recall the information. Then give an oral
response. Saying the answers aloud can reinforce[10] your memory and
understanding of the material.

ACTIVITY 10   Learning what sleep is

*With a partner, read the passage and underline the correct word in each
pair. Use a dictionary to help you with the meaning and pronunciation of
words. Then discuss the reading with your instructor.*

Sleep is a basic (biological / economical) state of rest for the mind
and body. During sleep, the eyes usually (open / close). The sleeping
person becomes (more / less) conscious. The body (increases / decreases)
in movement and responds (more / less) to the environment. Sleep is
controlled by the biological clock in the (brain / bones). This brain process

---

8. *deprivation* (*n.*) = the action of being *deprived*, or lacking things needed to be
   healthy or happy.
9. Maas, James. *Power Sleep* (Villard, 1998), as cited in
   http://www. sdearthtimes.com/et0298/et0298s12.html
10. *reinforce* (*tr.v.*) = to add strength to sthg., make it stronger.

has a 24-(hour / week) cycle. Its most important (function / consequence) is to control the daily cycle of (asleep / sleep) and wakefulness. The biological clock provides an (internal / external) wake-up signal to the rest of the brain. Ordinarily, this very powerful alerting signal occurs during the (daytime / nighttime) hours. This alerting signal keeps us (awake / drowsy).

The total amount of (sleep / sleepiness) that people need changes throughout the lifecycle. Infants and children sleep between 16 and 20 (minutes / hours) per day. Adults sleep between seven and (eight / eighteen) hours. (Teenagers / Adults) over 60 years of age sleep about six and a half hours.[10] Many people (deprive[11] / concentrate) their bodies of necessary sleep. This creates a sleep debt.

ACTIVITY 11   Understanding the main idea and details

In Part 1 of the lecture, the lecturer reviews material that students learned in the previous class.

Listen to the first part of the lecture. Choose the best response for each item.

1. The main idea of this part of the lecture is _____.

    a. A description of sleep

    b. A definition of sleep debt

    c. How to get a good night's sleep

2. All of the following are true statements. Circle the letters of the two details that the lecturer gives.

    a. Each of us has a specific daily sleep requirement.

    b. When we fall asleep, we can't perceive anything around us.

    c. The sleeping brain is an active brain.

    d. The biological clock controls our body temperature.

11. Nidus 2002; Rajput & Bromley, 1999, as cited by RN.com
12. *deprive* (*tr.v.*) = to prevent (sbdy./sthg.) from having; deny.

ACTIVITY 12 Focusing on questions

Lecturers ask questions for a lot of reasons. Some of them are . . .

- to find out what you know
- to make you think about something
- to check if you are following
- to see if you understand
- to get your permission or agreement
- to be friendly
- to wake you up

Can you think of other reasons for questions?

Listen to Part 1 of the lecture again. Raise your hand whenever you hear the lecturer ask a question. Your instructor will stop the recording when you raise your hand. Do you hear an oral response from the students in the class? With your instructor, discuss the lecturer's questions and students' responses. How does this interaction help students learn?

> Some lecturers like students to raise their hands before responding to questions. Others are more informal, and they prefer students to call out their responses at any time without raising their hands. Observe each classroom culture to see which way is acceptable.

ACTIVITY 13 Listening for main ideas

Listen to Parts 2 through 6 of the lecture. Try to catch the main idea of each part. (You will have a chance to listen to each part for details later.) Draw a line from each part to its main idea. Note: One sentence is not a main idea of this lecture.

Part 2	Americans don't get enough sleep.
	Sleep debt accumulates.
Part 3	
	Get up, walk around, and go and get a drink of water.
Part 4	
	Sleep debt is created when your body needs sleep.
Part 5	
	Drowsiness causes accidents.
Part 6	
	People do not realize that they are sleepy.

 ACTIVITY 14 Understanding an analogy

Master Student Tip

Use analogies to relate old and new information. Analogies relate similar concepts and ideas; use them to give you a picture of something familiar. Try to relate it to new information.

An analogy is a situation or story similar to another that helps people to understand. An analogy compares a familiar idea to an unfamiliar idea. People use analogies to help explain something or make it easier to understand.

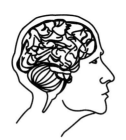

Analogy

The mind is like a muscle.

When you exercise it, it can perform better.

In Part 2, the lecturer uses an analogy. The comparison is between sleep debt and money debt.

Preview the sentences that follow. Then listen to Part 2 of the lecture again. Complete the sentences with the words in the right column. The first one is done for you.

1. Suppose you don't get _enough_ sleep?	body
2. What happens when you deprive your _____ and your brain the amount of sleep that it _____?	debt
	enough ✓
3. That creates a sleep _____.	owe
4. You _____ your body some sleep.	requires
5. Just like you're supposed to make your _____ payments every month.	100
	200
6. Say you're supposed to pay $_____ a month, but you pay only $_____.	300
	car
7. Then you're $_____ in debt.	payment
8. If you miss the _____ totally, then you're $300 in debt.	
9. _____ _____ is like that too.	injury
10. The bank can _____ _____ your car if you don't make any payments.	life
	take away
11. Sleep debt can take your _____ away if you're not careful,	sleep debt
12. It can cause serious _____ to your body.	

ACTIVITY 15 **Outlining main ideas and supporting details**

This lecturer uses data from research to support the main idea. Preview the sentences below. Then listen to Part 3 of the lecture again. Write phrases to complete the main idea and supporting details.

Main Point: Americans _____
Supporting details:

A. National Sleep Foundation surveyed _____ American adults. Results:

    1. Most Americans don't pay attention to recommendations (to do what?) _____ per night.

    2. On average, Americans sleep for _____ (< _____)
    (< is the symbol for *less than*: 2 < 25; > is the symbol for greater than: 17 > 4)

    3. 33 percent sleep for _____

    4. ⅓ sleep for < _____

B. Better Sleep Council study results: Half the people said

_____ the sleep they needed.

C. Gallup Poll survey results: _____ of the adult population

reports that _____ is a problem.

Conclusion: >_____ of all American adults are carrying

around _____

ACTIVITY **16** **Distinguishing main ideas from details**

Main ideas are larger, more important, and more general than details. Details are smaller and more specific. Details include facts and examples and usually support a main idea.

Listen to Parts 4–6 of the lecture again. Is each sentence below a main idea or a detail? Underline the appropriate phrase. The first one is done for you.

Part 4

1. <u>Main Idea</u>	Detail	Sleep debt is dangerous.
2. Main Idea	Detail	1 hr + 2 hr = 3 hrs sleep debt.
3. Main Idea	Detail	The larger the sleep debt you owe, the stronger your tendency to fall asleep in the daytime.
4. Main Idea	Detail	Even a loud noise can't keep you awake if you have a very large debt.

Part 5

5. Main Idea	Detail	Sleepy people function poorly, both physically and mentally.
6. Main Idea	Detail	Drivers who fall asleep at the wheel cause 1,500 deaths a year.
7. Main Idea	Detail	The bill for America's sleep debt is gigantic.

Part 6

8. Main Idea	Detail	Most people have no idea of how sleepy they are.
9. Main Idea	Detail	A third of the people were actually dangerously sleepy.
10. Main Idea	Detail	Maybe someone in this room is nodding off right now.
11. Main Idea	Detail	Drowsiness occurs just before you fall asleep.
12. Main Idea	Detail	A professor at Stanford made the class hold up red cards and shout, "Drowsiness is red alert![13]"
13. Main Idea	Detail	It's important to start repaying your sleep debt.

13. *red alert* (*n*) = a warning or alarm for an emergency situation, esp. for a fight or war.

▭ Using your Notes to Answer Questions

 ACTIVITY **17** Comprehending the lecture: True or False

You will hear eight statements about the lecture. Refer to your notes in Activities 11–16 and your auditory memory. After listening to each statement, circle True or False according your information.

1. True   False

2. True   False

3. True   False

4. True   False

5. True   False

6. True   False

7. True   False

8. True   False

9. True   False

10. True   False

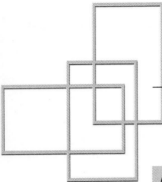

Part 2

EFFECTIVE ACADEMIC SPEAKING

ACTIVITY 18 Retelling the content of the lecture

To check your comprehension, a lecturer may ask you to summarize what you learned. Or you may find the information so interesting that you want to share it with a friend. Saying your responses aloud is one way to help you understand and remember the material.

Work in groups of three or four to retell the information in the lecture. Look at your notes in the previous activities. You do not need to remember the lecturer's exact words, but you must remember the ideas. Each student will retell one part at a time. Take turns as described below.

Speaker A: Retell the first part of the lecture to your group. Use your notes to remember the content.
Listeners: Remind the speaker of missing points by giving some keywords or ideas.

Speaker B: Retell the second part of the lecture to your group. Use your notes to remember the content.
Listeners: Remind the speaker of missing points by giving some keywords or ideas.

Speaker C: Retell the third part of the lecture to your group. Use your notes to remember the content.
Listeners: Remind the speaker of missing points by giving some keywords or ideas.

Continue in this way until your group has retold all five parts of the lecture at least twice. Retell a different part of the lecture each time it is your turn.

Your instructor may ask individual students to retell part of the lecture to the whole class.

ACTIVITY 19   Checking how well you retold the lecture

Answer the questions about yourself. Then discuss your answers with a partner.

1. Which parts of the lecture were easy for you to retell? Put a plus (+) by the easy parts. Put a minus (−) by the difficult parts. Tell why they were easy or difficult to retell.

   _____ Part 1: What is sleep?

   _____ Part 2: Sleep debt is created when your body needs sleep.

   _____ Part 3: Americans don't get enough sleep.

   _____ Part 4: Sleep debt accumulates.

   _____ Part 5: Drowsiness causes accidents.

   _____ Part 6: People do not realize that they are sleepy.

2. Which kind of information was easier for you to retell? Put a plus (+) by the easy part. Put a minus (−) by the difficult part. Tell why.

   _____ The main ideas

   _____ The supporting details

3. In what ways did you and your partner help each other retell the information accurately? Put a check (✔) by all the statements that are true.

   _____ I told my partners the missing or incorrect information that I read in my exercises on questions, answers, numbers, and key words.

   _____ I told my partners the missing or incorrect information that I recalled from my memory.

   _____ I gave my partners hints about the missing or incorrect information that I read in my notes.

   _____ I gave my partners hints about the missing or incorrect information that I recalled from my memory.

   _____ I asked my partners questions about the missing or incorrect information.

   _____ My partners retold everything perfectly. I did not need to help my partners.

   _____ I retold everything perfectly. My partners did not need to help me.

ACTIVITY 20 **Stressing and linking phrasal verbs**

Most phrasal verbs are stressed on the second word.

> **A:** What's <u>going ón</u>?
> **B:** The power just <u>went óut</u>.
> **A:** I didn't <u>shut dówn</u> my computer!
> **B:** <u>Shut</u> it <u>dówn</u> right awáy.

The ending sound of one word in the phrase is linked to the beginning sound of the next word.

> **A:** What is going ón?
> **B:** The power just went óut.
> **A:** I didn't shut dówn my computer!
> **B:** Shut it dówn right awáy.

Listen and pronounce the sentences above with proper phrase stress and linking.

Review the sentences in Activity 6. As you say the sentences, pay attention to phrase stress and linking.

ACTIVITY 21 **Using phrasal verbs in dialogues**

In conversing with others, it's important to pronounce sentences with good rhythm, stress, and linking. That makes it easier for others to understand you.

Complete the following dialogues. In the answer, say Yes. *Use the phrasal verb and a pronoun. Use the phrase in parentheses. Use good grammar. The first two answers are done for you.*

Listen to the dialogues. Check your answers and listen for rhythm, stress, and linking.

Practice the dialogues above with a partner. Speak with good rhythm, stress, and linking.

  1. A: Did they pay back their loan? (last month)

     B: Yes, they paid it back last month.

  2. A: Does she usually find out the answer? (always)

     B: Yes, she always finds it out.

3. A: Did you cut out chocolate from your diet? (last month)

B: _____

4. A: Does Bob shut his computer down at night? (every night)

B: _____

5. A: Does Carol fall asleep in the afternoon? (sometimes)

B: _____

6. A: Does this chapter deal with sleep? (certainly)

B: _____

7. A: Did you catch up on all of your homework? (yesterday)

B: _____

8. A: Did the students hand in their reports? (at the beginning of class)

B: _____

9. A: Did the teacher go over the last chapter? (before the new chapter)

B: _____

10. A: Did Mr. Lane wake up his son in the morning? (at 6:25)

B: _____

11. A: Does Ken talk about his girlfriend? (often)

B: _____

12. A: Are you with me? (of course)

B: _____

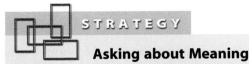

ACTIVITY 22   **Asking questions about meaning**

Discuss the following dialogues with your instructor.

> **STRATEGY**
>
> **Asking about Meaning**
>
> To ask about the meaning of a word or a concept, we use these sentence patterns:
>
> What does (any word) mean?
> What is the meaning of (any word)?
> What does it mean to (verb phrase)?
> What is a/an (noun phrase)?

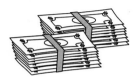

1. A: What does *accumulate* mean?
   B: Accumulate means to grow or increase in number over a period of time. Your money accumulates in your bank account if you don't use it all.

2. A: What is the meaning of *nod off*?
   B: It means to let your head fall forward and you fall asleep, like this. (Show how.)

3. A: What does it mean to *emphasize* something?
   B: It means to place importance on it, or stress it. You can emphasize something by saying it loudly or repeating it.

4. A: What is the *biological clock*?
   B: The biological clock is an internal mechanism that controls many body functions, such as temperature and awakening.

Make up questions about the words and phrases in the box. Refer to previous activities in this chapter. Use a dictionary as necessary. Afterwards, practice the dialogues with a partner. Speak with proper stress and linking. Continue to ask about the meanings of other words and phrases.

cut down on	expert	specific	sleep deprivation
enormous	pay back	recommend	tendency

1. A: _____

   B: It means to reduce or decrease. For example, I spend too much money. I need to cut down on my spending.

2. A: _____

   B: It means to repay. Suppose you borrow $20 from your friend. When you get your paycheck, you pay the money back.

3. A: _____

   B: It means exact, particular, or definite. My dad told me to wait in a specific place, under the oak tree in front of the post office.

4. A: _____

   B: Another way to say it is advise or suggest. If you like something or think it's good, you recommend it, like a restaurant, or a movie, or a class.

5. A: _____

   B: Oh, that's a person who knows a lot about something. It's someone with a high degree of skill or knowledge of a certain subject.

6. A: _____

   B: It is a large sleep debt. Scientists know it shortens your life and slows you down mentally.

7. A: _____

   B: It means very big, huge, gigantic! As a whole, Americans have an enormous sleep debt.

8. A: _____

   B: It is an inclination, a leaning in your attitude or your behavior. For example, I have a tendency to go to bed after midnight. My brother has a tendency to lose things.

 **ACTIVITY 23**   **Asking questions about differences**

> **STRATEGY**
>
> **Asking about Differences**
>
> To ask about the difference between two words, things or ideas, we use these sentence patterns:
>
> What's the difference between A and B?
> How are A and B different?

Discuss these model dialogues with your instructor.

1. **A:** What's the difference between *objective* and *subjective*?
    B: Objective is based on fact and not on someone's opinion. Subjective is based on someone's opinion or feelings. The researchers asked people if they felt sleepy. Their answers were subjective. The researchers measured how well they could do a task. Their measurements were objective.

2. **A:** What's the difference between *snoring* and *yawning*?
    B: Snoring is breathing noisily while asleep, like this (snore). Yawning is opening the mouth really wide and taking a deep breath, like this (yawn).

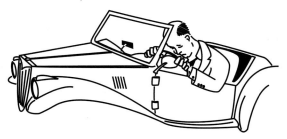

3. **A:** How are *sleepy* and *asleep* different?
    B: They're both adjectives, but *asleep* means already in a state of sleep, and *sleepy* means feeling drowsy and wanting to sleep.

4. **A:** What's the difference between *small* and *little*?
    B: Nothing. There's no difference between those two words. They're synonyms. They mean the same thing.

With a partner, create dialogues about differences using the following pairs of words. Refer to previous activities in this chapter. Use a dictionary as necessary. For #9, make your own question.

1. **A:** (blind and deaf) _____

   B: _____

2. **A:** (take away and go away) _____

   B: _____

3. **A:** (wake up and awaken) _____

   B: _____

4. **A:** (sleep and sleepiness) _____

   B: _____

5. **A:** (hand in and hand out) _____

   B: _____

6. **A:** (go to bed and go to sleep) _____

   B: _____

7. **A:** (lie down and get up) _____

   B: _____

8. **A:** (your sleep habits and mine) _____

   B: _____

9. **A:** (your own question) _____

   B: _____

Practice the dialogues above with a partner. Speak with proper stress and linking. Afterwards, continue to ask about the differences between other things.

ACTIVITY 24   Determining how sleepy you are

Are you awake or asleep—or somewhere in between?

A person's ability to stay awake or fall asleep at any particular time depends on many factors. One of these factors is the time of day. Another factor is what you are doing at the time. for example, lying down rather than standing up increases your likelihood of falling asleep.

Awake

Sleepy

Asleep

The questions on the next page help measure your degree of daytime sleepiness or average sleep propensity.[14] First, discuss the questions and choices with your instructor. Ask questions about words and ideas that are not clear to you. Then complete the survey personally.

14. *propensity (n.)* = a tendency

The Epworth Sleepiness Scale[15]

How likely are you to doze off or fall asleep in the following situations, in contrast to feeling just tired? This refers to your usual way of life in recent times. Even if you have not done some of these things recently, imagine how they would have affected you. Use the following scale to choose the most appropriate number for each situation.

Activity	Would never doze	Slight chance of dozing	Moderate chance of dozing	High chance of dozing
1. Sitting and reading	0	1	2	3
2. Watching TV	0	1	2	3
3. Sitting, inactive in a public place: e.g., a theater or a meeting	0	1	2	3
4. As a passenger in a car for an hour without a break	0	1	2	3
5. Lying down to rest in the afternoon when circumstances permit	0	1	2	3
6. Sitting and talking to someone	0	1	2	3
7. Sitting quietly after a lunch without alcohol	0	1	2	3
8. In a car, while stopped for a few minutes in traffic	0	1	2	3

Make sure that you circled a number for each activity above. Then add up all of the numbers you circled and write the number below.

My sleepiness score = _____

Turn to the next page to find out what your sleepiness score means.

15. This measure is used with permission from Dr. Murray Johns, of the Epworth Sleep Centre in Melbourne, Australia.

The Epworth Sleepiness Scale: Basic Interpretation

0–10 This is the normal range for adults who do not have a chronic sleep disorder (including snoring).

Important:

If you have trouble sleeping, or if your score is 11 or higher, you need to seek advice from a sleep professional.[16]

 ACTIVITY **25** **Getting the most value from your sleep**

Good sleep habits affect many aspects of your life, for example, your education, your work, your family, and your social life. Make sleep a priority, and your good health will help you.

Preview the following recommendations about how to get the most value from your sleep. Then listen to the sleep tips. You will hear the passage three times. Fill in the missing words, one word per blank. Afterwards, discuss the information. Ask questions about meaning, pronunciation, and spelling.

1. Do you want to know how to get the most value from your sleep?

I'm going to give you some tips from the sleep _____.

These tips are from _____ who have done a great deal of

research on the effect of sleep on the human body.

2. First of all, they _____ keeping regular hours. Do any of

you like to _____ _____ late on the weekends,

compared to weekday nights? Well, that upsets your biological

_____. For better sleep, try to _____

_____ _____ at the same time each night and

wake up _____ _____ _____

_____ each morning—even on weekends.

16. The result of this self-assessment is not intended to replace medical advice. Information from this self-assessment must not be misinterpreted as an attempt to diagnose, treat, cure, or prevent any disease. Snoring and other sleep disorders, especially sleep apnea, can lead to serious problems, including heart attacks and strokes.

3. Now, here's _____ _____ _____
_____ I'm sure you'll hear from other sources besides
sleep experts, and that's to _____ regularly. Some form of
exercise for 20 to 30 minutes _____ _____
three days a week is ideal—but be sure not to exercise
_____ _____ to bedtime.

4. _____ _____ _____ _____
drink coffee, or tea, or soft drinks with caffeine in them—or eat
chocolate? Then you may be familiar with this one: _____
_____ _____ caffeine and other stimulants.
Consuming stimulants such as caffeine in the _____
makes it harder to fall asleep. Caffeine also prevents _____
_____ and may make you wake up in the middle of the
night more often. If you're having trouble _____
_____, you may want to cut out these stimulants
altogether.

5. If you drink alcohol, drink only in moderation— _____
_____ _____ a day or less. Drinking alcohol
before bed makes it _____ to stay asleep, interrupts the
sleep stages and can _____ _____
_____ _____ in the early-morning hours.
Again, if you're having trouble falling asleep, you _____
_____ to cut out alcohol altogether.

6. What about the bed you sleep on? _____ _____
_____ _____ on a good bed. If your mattress is
too small, too soft, _____ _____, or too old, it's
difficult to get deep, restful sleep. It won't provide the comfort and
support you need to _____ _____. Also, don't
use your bedroom as an _____. Use your bedroom for
sleeping.

7. Don't smoke. You've _____ heard this advice for other
reasons. But _____ have also found out that smoking has
negative effects on sleeping. Smokers take longer to fall asleep, they
_____ _____ _____, and they spend
less time in deep sleep.

8. If you're tired, _____ _____ _____
early, or sleep later in the morning, or take naps. If you feel
_____ while driving, pull off the road into a safe area as
soon as possible and _____ _____
_____. Set your watch to awaken you in _____
minutes.

9. What should you do _____ _____ to bed?
Unwind and relax. If you have had a busy day, it's good to end the
day _____ _____ _____ before
bedtime. Try to deal with any _____ and distractions
before going to bed. It is possible to do this _____
_____ in a journal, by doing some light reading, by
listening _____ _____ _____, by
taking a warm bath, or by drinking a small glass of _____
_____. Think about your successes of the day.
_____ and unwind.

10. These are just a few _____ made by sleep experts. There are more, especially for people who _____ from specific sleep disorders.

11. Probably _____ _____ _____ piece of advice is this: make sleep a high priority, a really important part of every day. Say "yes" to sleep even when you're tempted to _____ _____ _____. You'll thank yourself _____ _____ _____. If you already have _____ _____ _____ , you should _____ _____ _____ just as soon as you can.

12. If you follow these tips, you'll be _____ _____ _____ the best sleep you need.

ACTIVITY 26 Participating in a jigsaw dictation

You have read and discussed many tips about getting the most value from your sleep. Now you will take part in a jigsaw activity. Follow these steps.

Round one: learn the sentences

Your instructor will divide the class into two, three, four or six groups. Each group will get a letter name: A, B, C, etc. Your instructor will hand out the script of one portion of the sleep tips in the previous activity. Each group is responsible for helping its members learn. You must learn the correct pronunciation of your group's sentences. Discuss the content, meaning, and vocabulary with your partners. Practice pronouncing your sleep tips until you can say them fluently.

Round two: dictate the sentences

Now you will form new groups. Each new group should consist of a member of each previous group (e.g., one A, one B, one C, etc). Dictate the sleep tips you practiced with the first group to the partners in your new group. Dictate the sentences in order. Use good pronunciation and speak fluently. Your new partners will write the dictated sentences. Listeners, ask the speaker for repetition and clarification as necessary.

ACTIVITY 27 Checking your participation in dictation

Answer the questions about yourself. Then discuss your answers with a partner.

1. Round One: In what ways did you and your partners help each other learn the information? Put a check (✓) by all the statements that are true.

    _____ I explained the meaning of a word or phrase.

    _____ I told my partner which word to stress in a sentence.

    _____ I told my partner which syllable to stress in a word.

    _____ I modeled the correct pronunciation of words and phrases.

    _____ My partner(s) explained the meaning of a word or phrase.

    _____ My partner(s) told me which word to stress in a sentence.

    _____ My partner(s) told me which syllable to stress in a word.

    _____ My partner(s) modeled the correct pronunciation of words and phrases.

2. Round Two: Which was easier? Put a check (✓) by one of the following sentences.

    _____ Dictating the sentences aloud to my partners was easier for me.

    _____ Listening and writing the sentences (or words) was easier for me.

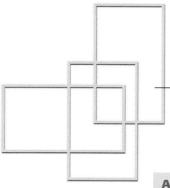

Part 3

ASSESSING YOUR LISTENING AND SPEAKING SKILLS

ACTIVITY 28 Applying information and skills from the chapter

Some of the following questions will help you review the information about sleep and sleep debt, and you will connect the information to your own sleep habits. Many of the questions will help you review language skills. These types of questions may be on a test.

Your instructor may ask you to discuss these questions in a group, write down the answers to the questions, or record your oral answers to the questions.

1. What are the three to four most important pieces of information about sleep that you learned from this chapter?

   _____

   _____

   _____

   _____

2. Which three tips are the most helpful for you to get better sleep?

   _____

   _____

   _____

3. Think of a specific person (e.g., a brother, your mother, a co-worker). Write the person's name here: _____
   Which two sleep tips would you recommend to him/her?

   _____

   _____

4. Write three different questions to ask about the meaning of the word *accumulate*. Then write an answer.

_____

_____

_____

_____

5. Write two different questions to ask about the difference between the words *huge* and *enormous*. Then write an answer.

_____

_____

_____

6. Circle the number of the best phrase to complete each sentence about phrasal verbs.

   a. If a phrasal verb is separable (*hand in*), put the noun object (*homework*) _____.

   (1) after the particle   (2) between the verb and the particle
   (3) either; it does not matter

   b. If a phrasal verb is separable (*hand in*), put the pronoun object (*it*) _____.

   (1) after the particle   (2) between the verb and the particle
   (3) either; it does not matter

   c. If a phrasal verb is inseparable (*deal with*), put the noun object (*sleep debt*) _____.

   (1) after the particle   (2) between the verb and the particle
   (3) either; it does not matter

   d. If a phrasal verb is inseparable (*deal with*), put the pronoun object (*it*) _____.

   (1) after the particle   (2) between the verb and the particle
   (3) either; it does not matter

   e. Most phrasal verbs are stressed on the _____ word.

   (1) first   (2) second   (3) third   (4) any; it does not matter

f. Write the phrasal verb synonym for each one-word verb below. Write S for separable or I for inseparable. Then write a sentence using the phrasal verb.

One-Word Verb	Phrasal Verb	S/I
discover	_____	___
recover, finish	_____	___
repay	_____	___
handle, manage	_____	___
remove; stop	_____	___
remain awake	_____	___
close completely	_____	___
discuss	_____	___
withdraw, remove	_____	___
reduce, decrease	_____	___
awaken	_____	___

🎧 **ACTIVITY 29** **Reviewing pronunciation, stress, and fluency**

Review these words and dialogues. Write the syllable-stress code for words 1–10. Draw intonation lines over the keywords in dialogues 11–14. Then practice with a partner. Pronounce each item as clearly and fluently as you can. Have your partner listen and help you with your pronunciation of syllables, stress, and intonation. Take turns. Your instructor may ask you to record your pronunciation of these items and others in this chapter.

1. economy [——-——]   6. specific [——-——]
2. function [——-——]   7. recommend [——-——]
3. perceive [——-——]   8. emphasize [——-——]
4. process [——-——]   9. internal [——-——]
5. research [——-——]   10. stimulation [——-——]

11. **A:** Did you submit your homework?
    B: Yes, I already handed it in.
12. **A:** Can you remember to shut down the computer?
    B: Yes, I'll shut it down in ten minutes.
13. **A:** What are you doing this weekend?
    B: I must catch up on my sleep.
14. **A:** I'm full of anxiety and tenseness.
    B: Try to deal with your worries before bedtime.

ACTIVITY 30 **Hearing syllables and word stress**

Listen carefully to ten words from the chapter. You will hear each word once. Listen for the number of syllables and the stressed syllable. Write the syllable-stress code in the brackets.

Example: You hear the word **accident.** [_3_-_|_]

1. [——-——]   5. [——-——]   8. [——-——]
2. [——-——]   6. [——-——]   9. [——-——]
3. [——-——]   7. [——-——]   10. [——-——]
4. [——-——]

ACTIVITY 31 Taking dictation

In this dictation, you will hear vocabulary and sentence patterns that you practiced in this chapter. Your instructor will tell you the number of words in each sentence. Write the numbers within the parentheses and use them as a guide. You will hear each sentence three times. First, listen and try to understand the meaning of the whole sentence. Second, listen and write. Third, listen and check.

1. _____ (____ words)

   _____

2. _____ (____ words)

   _____

3. _____ (____ words)

   _____

4. _____ (____ words)

   _____

5. _____ (____ words)

   _____

6. _____ (____ words)

   _____

7. _____ (____ words)

   _____

8. _____ (____ words)

   _____

ACTIVITY 32 Summarizing your progress

How well can you perform the following objectives?

I can . . .	Barely	Somewhat	Fairly well	Very well
Use vocabulary and expressions to discuss sleep.				
Use a dictionary to learn the pronunciation of new words.				
Pronounce key vocabulary with proper syllables and word stress.				
Use phrasal verbs with proper meaning, phrase stress, and linking.				
Understand an analogy.				
Distinguish main ideas from details.				
Ask questions about meaning.				
Ask questions about differences.				
Ask and answer questions about sleep and human behavior.				
Relate the contents of the lecture to my own sleep habits.				
Take dictation of sentences related to sleep.				

WEB POWER

You will find additional exercises related to the content in this chapter at http://esl.college.hmco.com/students.

Laughter Is the Best Medicine

ACADEMIC FOCUS: SCIENCE AND SOCIAL SCIENCE ▶
PSYCHOLOGY, SOCIOLOGY, AND MEDICINE

Academic Listening and Speaking Objectives

In this chapter, you will hear a lecture that an instructor gives about laughter. You will pronounce academic vocabulary and discuss topics related to laughter, physiology, psychology, and health. You will participate in listening, speaking, and thinking activities. In particular,
you will:

- Develop vocabulary and expressions related to laughter
- Use a dictionary to learn the pronunciation of academic words
- Hear, identify, and pronounce key vocabulary with proper syllables and word stress
- Predict the content of a lecture
- Identify and use transitions for introducing a paraphrase or an explanation: *In other words, that is, I mean*
- Recognize the relationship between main ideas and examples
- Understand the significance of an extended example
- Understand and use tag questions with falling intonation
- Watch a comedy and identify humorous elements
- Present a report on a comedy
- Relate the contents of the lecture to laughter in your life
- Take dictation of sentences related to laughter

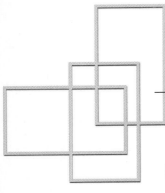

Part 1

▭ Getting Ready for the Lecture

Human beings love to laugh. Laughter lightens life from childhood through adulthood into old age. We love to laugh so much that there are industries that focus on laughter. Comedians tell jokes and funny stories. Clowns wear colorful makeup and funny costumes. Artists draw humorous comics. Actors in situation comedies[1] say and do things that amuse us and make us laugh. We also laugh for other reasons. In fact, laughter is actually a complex response. In this lecture you will learn about the relationship of laughter to your body, your mind, and your friends.

ACTIVITY 1 Discussing what makes you laugh

Discuss the question patterns and vocabulary with your instructor. Then, in a small group of three or four students, ask each other questions and discuss your responses.

1. Do you laugh at _____? Or Do(es) _____ make you laugh?

    clowns
    comedians
    sitcoms
    movies
    books
    stories
    comics
    jokes
    tickling
    hearing someone laugh
    seeing something strange (If so, what?)

1. *situation comedy*, also called *sitcom* (*n. phr.*) = a television comedy series in which a regular cast of characters, usually working or living together, respond to everyday situations in a humorous way

2. When do you laugh more, _____ or _____?

   in your native language/in English
   with your friends/with your family
   with people you know/with strangers
   alone/with other people
   in the daytime/at nighttime
   at school/at home
   at work/at school
   during a party/during class
   when you're happy/when you're sad
   when someone tickles your feet/your neck
   when you tell something funny/hear something funny

3. Do you have the same sense of humor[2] as others in your family? Explain.

▭ Looking at Language

ACTIVITY 2 Identifying syllables and word stress

Listen to the pronunciation of these words. Clap or tap the number of syllables you hear. Then write the syllable-stress code. The first one is done for you.

cell (*n.*)   [_|_ - _|_]   efficiently (*adv.*) [___ - ___]

comfortable (*adj.*)   [___ - ___]   examine (*vt.*)   [___ - ___]

confidence (*n.*)   [___ - ___]   humorous (*adj.*) [___ - ___]

connection (*n.*)   [___ - ___]   physiology (*n.*)   [___ - ___]

contagious (*adj.*)   [___ - ___]   profession (*n.*)   [___ - ___]

decrease (*tr.v., intr.v.*)[___ - ___]   relieve (*tr.v.*)   [___ - ___]

defend (*vt.*)   [___ - ___]

After you mark the syllable-stress code, take turns saying the words to your partner. Pronounce each word with the correct number of syllables. Make the stressed syllable long, strong, and high. Hear and feel the beats by clapping as you pronounce. Help your partner pronounce the words with correct syllables and stress.

2. *sense of humor* (*n. phr.*) = an ability to understand or appreciate humor

ACTIVITY 3 Taking dictation

You will hear the words in Activity 2 in context. You will hear each sentence three times. First, listen and try to understand the meaning of the whole sentence. Second, listen and write. Third, listen and check. Use the number of words in the parentheses as a guide.

1. _____ (10 words)

2. _____ (8 words)

3. _____ (6 words)

4. _____ (8 words)

5. _____ (12 words)

6. _____ (8 words)

7. _____ (6 words)

8. _____ (6 words)

9. _____ (7 words)

10. _____ (10 words)

11. _____ (6 words)

12. _____ (7 words)

ACTIVITY 4   **Matching words with definitions**

Write each word next to its definition.

cell (*n.*)	contagious (*adj.*)	humorous (*adj.*)
comfortable (*adj.*)	decrease (*tr.v., intr.v.*)	physiology (*n.*)
confidence (*n.*)	defend (*tr.v.*)	profession (*n.*)
connection (*n.*)	efficiently (*adv.*)	relieve (*tr.v.*)
	examine (*tr.v.*)	

1. _____ To make or keep (sbdy./sthg.) safe from attack or harm; guard.

2. _____ To look at (sbdy./sthg.) closely and carefully; inspect or study.

3. _____ Funny, comical, amusing.

4. _____ Productively, economically.

5. _____ To become smaller in number; to reduce.

6. _____ A belief in your ability to succeed; trust; faith.

7. _____ A relationship (between people, actions, ideas).

8. _____ Relaxed and restful, free from stress or anxiety.

9. _____ The scientific study of living bodies (humans, animals, plants) and how they work.

10. _____ The smallest and most basic unit of living things.

11. _____ An occupation that requires training and specialized study.

12. _____ To lessen or reduce (pain or anxiety, for example); ease.

13. _____ Capable of being given to others through physical contact or by air.

ACTIVITY 5 **Learning the vocabulary of academic lectures**

Look up each academic word in an English dictionary. Copy the pronunciation of each word exactly. Use the part of speech to guide you to the right entry. Write the syllable-stress code. Study the definition. Then compare your answers with a classmate's. The first one is done for you.

1. approach
   (*tr.v.*)

   ap·proach   (ə-prōch´)   [_2_ - _2_]

   To begin to deal with or work on sthgs.

2. benefit
   (*n.*)

   _____ _____ [___ - ___]

   Sthg. that is of help; an advantage.

3. bond
   (*intr.v.*)

   _____ _____ [___ - ___]

   To form a close personal relationship, to become friends.

4. consist of
   (*phr. v. insep.*)

   _____ _____ [___ - ___]

   To be made up of (syn.), to be composed of.

5. contract
   (*tr.v.*)

   _____ _____ [___ - ___]

   To make sthg. smaller by drawing together.

6. design
   (*tr.v.*)

   _____ _____ [___ - ___]

   To intend sthg. for a particular purpose; to make sthg. in a skillful or artistic way.

7. detect
   (*tr.v.*)

   _____ _____ [___ - ___]

   To notice, observe, discover the existence of sthg./sbdy.

8. medical
   (*adj.*)

   _____ _____ [___ - ___]

   Related to medicine (the science of studying, treating, and preventing diseases and disorders of the body).

9. negative
   (*adj.*)

   _____ _____ [___ - ___]

   Not helpful; not positive; expressing refusal.

10. positive   _____   _____   [___ - ___]
    (*adj.*)

    Helpful, hopeful, optimistic, beneficial.

11. role   _____   _____   [___ - ___]
    (*n.*)

    A character or part played by an actor or actress.

12. sociology   _____   _____   [___ - ___]
    (*n.*)

    The scientific study of human social relationships
    and behavior of individuals and groups in society.

13. survive   _____   _____   [___ - ___]
    (*intr.v.*)

    To stay alive or exist, especially under difficult
    conditions.

14. vary   _____   _____   [___ - ___]
    (*intr.v.*)

    To be different from others of its type.

    _____   _____   [___ - ___]

    variety (*n.*) A particular type or kind within a
    general group.

15. vibrate   _____   _____   [___ - ___]
    (*intr.v.*)

    To shake or move back and forth quickly.

ACTIVITY 6   **Pronouncing the academic vocabulary**

Listen to the pronunciation of each word in the previous activity. Check the syllable-stress code.

Pronounce each word with your instructor or the recording, and then practice with a partner.

ACTIVITY 7 Listening to the academic vocabulary in context

Listen to the sentences and complete each one with a word from the academic word list in Activity 5. Sometimes you will hear different forms of the words on the list. Write the form that you hear.

1. The sense of humor _____ among individuals.

2. Television sitcoms are _____ to make people laugh.

3. Charlie Chaplin played the _____ of a clown known as The Tramp in more than 70 films.

4. Your body _____ about 50 million cells, including T-cells to fight infections.

5. We will learn about the _____ of laughter on the immune system.

6. When you have a muscle spasm, all of the fibers _____.

7. A physiologist studies physiology, a _____ doctor studies medicine, a psychologist studies psychology, and a sociologist studies _____.

8. They may _____ the same problem from different angles.

9. A metal detector can _____ metal objects such as coins and jewelry.

10. _____ stress is harmful to your health, but _____ stress is beneficial.

11. Luckily, she _____ the automobile crash.

12. The coach held a party so that the teammates could _____ with each other.

13. As he played the violin, the strings _____.

☐ Getting Information from the Lecture

 **ACTIVITY** **8** Predicting the content of the lecture

STRATEGY

Learning to Make Predictions

Good listeners make predictions[3] about what they are going to hear in a lecture. They prepare in many ways. For example, they read the textbook and complete written assignments before the lecture. They recognize the pronunciation and understand the meaning of vocabulary related to the topic. They are familiar with many English grammar and sentence patterns. They bring their own background knowledge about the topic. They think about what they have to learn about the topic to do well in the course.

Read the phrases in the box. Predict the content that might be in the lecture about laughter. Put a check (✓) next to each one.

_____ History of laughter

_____ Introduction

_____ Medical effects of laughter

_____ Jokes

_____ Dangerous effects of laughter

_____ Laughter around the world

_____ Psychological effects of laughter

_____ Physiological description of laughter

_____ Laughter and politics

_____ Sociological effects of laughter

3. *prediction* (*n.*) = a statement of what you think will happen in the future

ACTIVITY 9 Getting an overview of a lecture

Listen to the entire lecture. Try to get an overview.⁴ Refer to the phrases in the previous activity. Some of them are main ideas in the lecture. Write those below in the order that you hear them. You may listen more than once.

1. _____

2. _____

3. _____

4. _____

5. _____

ACTIVITY 10 Understanding the introduction

Sometimes an instructor begins the body of a lecture right away. Other times an instructor begins by reviewing a homework assignment or a previous lecture. Many give a preview of the main ideas of the lecture that they are going to present. Some ask students questions to prompt them to think about the topic. Others tell a story or a joke or quote a well-known saying.⁵ Still others may do something unusual or surprising to get the attention of the audience.

On the next page, read the list of teaching methods. Listen to Part 1 of the lecture again. Put a check (✓) next to the methods that the lecturer uses in this part.

Listen to the same part of the lecture again. Jot down notes about details on the blank lines. Then discuss your results with your classmates.

4. *overview* (*n.*) = a general picture of something, a summary
5. *saying* (*n.*) = an expression or short sentence that is wise, common and familiar to many people; a proverb: *An apple a day keeps the doctor away.*

The Lecturer...	Notes
_____ Goes over a homework assignment.	_____ _____
_____ Reviews a previous lecture.	_____ _____
_____ Does something unusual or surprising.	_____ _____
_____ Asks students questions about the topic.	_____ _____
_____ Tells a joke.	_____ _____
_____ Quotes a saying.	_____ _____
_____ Gives a preview of the main ideas of the lecture.	_____ _____
_____ Gives instructions on a new assignment.	_____ _____

 **Using transitions to introduce a paraphrase**

STRATEGY

Understanding Paraphrases

A speaker may paraphrase or explain a word or concept to make it easier to understand, especially if it is new or difficult. Sometimes a transition phrase is used before the concept is paraphrased or explained. Here are some transitions used in other lectures in this book.

Master Student Tip

Listen for phrases that paraphrase or explain important concepts. If you hear a transition like *that is,* or *in other words,* you can expect to hear two ways to understand the concepts.

Discuss the sentences below with your instructor. Then mark the sentences. Draw a box around the transitions. Underline the synonymous phrases. Draw an arrow from the second synonym to the first. The first item is done for you as an example.

1. How many meals will you have consumed in your lifetime? I mean, altogether in your whole life? (Ch. 2 Nutrition)

   Transition: *I mean*
   Synonymous phrases: in your whole life means in your lifetime
   Understand it visually:
   How many meals will you have consumed in your lifetime? I mean, altogether in your whole life?

2. One important point for you to keep in mind now is this: a well-chosen diet, that is, your choice of foods—your diet—will keep you healthy. (Ch. 2 Nutrition)

   Transition: *that is*
   Synonymous phrases: *choice of foods* means *diet*

3. A nutrient is an ingredient in your diet that has nutritious qualities; in other words, it nourishes or promotes growth. (Ch. 2 Nutrition)

   Transition: *in other words*
   Synonymous phrases: *nourishes or promotes growth* means *has nutritious qualities*

4. Geography is more than the study of the land. What I mean to say is, geography is the study of land and people. (Ch. 3 Geography)

   Transition: *What I mean to say is*
   Explanatory phrase: the study of land and people tells more about more than the study of the land

5. Sleep is a state of complete perceptual disengagement from the environment. That means we can't perceive anything around us. (Ch. 4 Sleep)

   Transition: *That means*
   Explanatory phrase: we can't perceive anything around us explains a state of complete perceptual disengagement from the environment

Sometimes a speaker paraphrases or explains something without a transition phrase.

6. Music stirs people's emotions, their feelings; it moves them emotionally. (Ch. 1 Music)

   Transition: *none*
   First synonymous phrase: *feelings* means *emotions*
   Second synonymous phrase: it moves them emotionally means music stirs people's emotions

7. Sleep debt doesn't go away. No way! It grows. It accumulates. The sleep that you lose on successive nights increases progressively as a larger and larger sleep debt. (Ch. 4 Sleep)

   Transition: *none*
   Explanatory phrase: *grows* expands on *doesn't go away*
   Synonymous phrase: *accumulates* means *grows*
   Summary sentence: The sleep that you lose on successive nights increases progressively as a larger and larger sleep debt. It (sleep debt) accumulates.

In Part 1 of the lecture, the speaker uses transitions in the sentences below. As you listen for the fourth time, write the transition in the box. Write the paraphrase in the blank. Then underline the synonymous part of the sentence before the transition.

I mean   that is   in other words

8. No laughing allowed. [   ], _____

9. Some scientists approach laughter from a physiological point of view,

   [   ], _____

10. Other researchers approach it from a psychological point of view,

    [   ], _____

The lecturer does not use transitions before all of the paraphrases. In the following sentences, there is no transition. Write the keywords in the paraphrase in the blank. Then underline the synonymous part of the sentence before the transition.

11. Still others approach this topic from a sociological viewpoint—

    _____

12. And people in the health profession approach laughter from a medical

    viewpoint—_____

ACTIVITY 12   Focusing on details in an outline

Listen to Part 2 of the lecture again. In this part, the lecturer presents a physiological description of laughter. Listen for facts that support the main ideas. Complete the outline with the phrases in the box. The first blank is filled in for you.

II. Physiological description of laughter	
A. Laughter ≠ humor	**A.** something funny (joke)
1. Laughter: _____	a response to humor
2. Humor: _____	≠ (is not equal to)

B. Brain pressures you to conduct two activities at once

   1. Set of _____

      a. Smile requires _____ to contract big muscle

   2. Production of a _____

      a. Get _____ in your diaphragm

      b. Spasms _____ through the epiglottis

      c. Result: _____ sound

B. 15 small muscles
   sound
   gestures
   spasms
   ha-ha-ha-ha
   force air out

C. Many parts of the body work to make a laugh.

   1. Lungs _____

   2. Oxygen level in your blood _____

   3. _____ and blood pressure go up

   4. Eyes water

   5. Mouth _____ rapidly

   6. Muscle spasms in your _____

C. increases
   heart rate
   work harder
   opens and closes
   arms, trunk, legs

D. The sound of human laughter has a certain form.

   1. Basic form consists of _____

      repeated every _____ milliseconds

   2. We can laugh _____

   3. We can't laugh _____

D. ha-ha-ha
   ha-ho-ha-ho
   short, vowel-like
    notes
   210

E. Laughter is _____.

   1. _____ mechanism in brain

   2. Laughter causes _____

   3. You laugh— _____ laugh too.

E. laugh detector
   more laughter
   contagious
   others around
    you

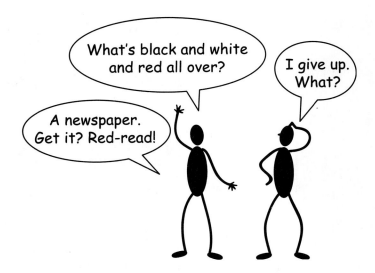

 ACTIVITY 13 **Listening for examples**

Listen to Part 3 of the lecture again. In this part, the lecturer discusses the sociological effects of laughter. Listen for examples and other supporting details. Complete the outline with the phrases in the box.

III. Sociological effects of laughter	
A. People laugh at different things.	**A.** cartoons jokes comedy shows

1. Things that are designed to make people laugh:
 	
       _____, riddles,[6] humorous stories,
 	
       slapstick, _____, TV sitcoms,
 	
       _____
	- - - - - - -
	 foolish
	 age
	 surprising

2. Actions: ridiculous, _____, silly, _____, unexpected	
3. Topics depending on _____ or interests	
4. Themselves	

6. *riddle* (*n.*) = a question or a puzzle that requires clever thought to answer or understand

B. Sense of _____ varies.

   1. Among _____

   2. Changes from childhood to _____

   3. Differs from one _____ to another

B. adulthood
humor
culture
individuals

C. Purpose of laughter is to make human

_____

   1. Laugh more with _____ than strangers

   2. Laugh more when you feel _____

   3. Laugh _____ more with others than alone.

   4. Laughter = form of _____

C. comfortable
friends
30 times
social
  bonding
connections

ACTIVITY 14   Listening to an extended example

In this part of the lecture, the speaker tells the story of a specific person. Then he continues with facts from research. Below are some questions to help you think about the medical effects of laughter.

With your instructor, preview the questions. Ask about words that you do not understand. Then listen to Part 4 again. Think about the connection between the extended example—the story—and the main points of this part of the lecture. As you listen, jot down notes to answer these questions.

A. The Story

1. Who is Patch Adams?

   _____

2. What happened to him in medical school?

   _____

   _____

3. What unusual things did he do as a doctor in a hospital?

   _____

   _____

4. How did the patients react to him?

_____

_____

_____

B. The Immune System

1. What is the relationship between the immune system and bacteria, microbes, viruses, toxins, and parasites?

_____

_____

_____

2. Why are people under stress more likely to develop infectious diseases?

_____

_____

_____

3. What can positive stress do for a person?

_____

_____

_____

C. Laughter Has Numerous Benefits

1. What happens to your T-cells, which fight infections?

_____

_____

2. What happens to your blood pressure?

_____

_____

3. What happens to your muscles?

_____

_____

4. What happens to your lungs?

_____

_____

The Connection

What is the significance of this story to the lecturer's main point?

_____

_____

 ACTIVITY 15   Distinguishing main ideas from details

Main ideas are larger, more important, and more general than details. Details are smaller and more specific. Details include facts and examples. Details usually support a main idea.

Listen to Part 5 of the lecture again. This part is about the psychological effects of laughter. Is each sentence below a main idea or a detail? Underline the appropriate phrase. The first one is done for you.

1. <u>Main Idea</u>   Detail   Laughter is good for your mental health.

2. Main Idea   Detail   You don't worry about the past or future.

3. Main Idea   Detail   Laughter has benefits for laughers and others near laughers.

4. Main Idea   Detail   Patients build confidence, self-esteem, and hope through laughter.

5. Main Idea   Detail   There are more than ninety laughter clubs in Bangalore, India.

6. Main Idea   Detail   Laughter improves your immune system, builds muscles, and relieves stress.

 ACTIVITY 16   Listening to the whole lecture

Listen to the entire lecture from beginning to end. As you listen this time, apply what you learned in the previous activities to the whole lecture.

☐ Using Your Notes to Answer Questions

ACTIVITY 17 Checking your comprehension

Read each sentence and underline the correct phrase to complete it accurately. Refer to your notes in Activities 9–15.

1. Laughter is _____ humor.
   - **a.** a form of
   - **b.** a cause of
   - **c.** a response to

2. Compared to a smile, a laugh requires _____ muscles.
   - **a.** fewer
   - **b.** more
   - **c.** the same number of

3. To laugh, you have to _____.
   - **a.** move your body
   - **b.** make a sound
   - **c.** produce movement and sound

4. During laughter, your heart rate _____.
   - **a.** increases
   - **b.** decreases
   - **c.** stays the same

5. Laughter is _____ physical exercise.
   - **a.** a form of
   - **b.** a cause of
   - **c.** a response to

6. The basic form of a laugh consists of _____.
   - **a.** ha-ha-ha-ha sounds
   - **b.** 210 milliseconds
   - **c.** short, vowel-like notes

7. We _____ laugh at the same things.
   a. all   **b.** don't all   **c.** never

8. Laughter is contagious, that is, _____.
   a. it is a disease   **b.** friends share it easily   **c.** researchers study it

9. Laughter is a/an _____ activity.
   a. individual   **b.** social   **c.** institutional

10. Dr. Patch Adams wore clown clothes to the hospital because _____.
    a. he was childish and happy   **b.** he wanted to make his patients laugh   **c.** he tried to make the hospital staff happy

11. The patients at the hospital _____.
    a. tried to change the health care system   **b.** played jokes and made people laugh   **c.** laughed, felt hopeful, and got better

12. The immune system is a _____ against germs.
    a. defense mechanism   **b.** laugh detector   **c.** psychological mechanism

13. The more you laugh, _____.
    a. the higher your blood pressure goes   **b.** the lower your oxygen level gets   **c.** the more active your T-cells become

14. Laughter _____ mental health.
    a. benefits   **b.** requires   **c.** causes

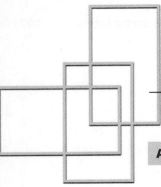

Part 2

EFFECTIVE ACADEMIC SPEAKING

ACTIVITY 18 Retelling the content of a lecture

Retelling helps you review and remember what you learned. When you retell, you recall information and think about the connections between main ideas and supporting details, between major and minor details. Retelling also benefits your classmates. It helps them get information that they missed.

Work in groups of three or four to retell the information in the lecture. Look at your notes in the previous activities. You do not need to remember the lecturer's exact words, but you must remember the ideas. Each student retells one part at a time. Take turns as described below.

Speaker A:	Retell the first part of the lecture. Use your notes to remember the content.
Listeners:	Remind the speaker of missing points by giving some keywords or ideas.
Speaker B:	Retell the second part of the lecture. Use your notes to remember the content.
Listeners:	Remind the speaker of missing points by giving some keywords or ideas.
Speakers C, D:	Continue in this way until your group has retold all five parts of the lecture at least twice. Retell a different part of the lecture each time it is your turn.

Your instructor may ask individual students to retell part of the lecture to the whole class.

ACTIVITY 19 Checking how well you retold the lecture

Answer the questions about yourself. Then discuss your answers with a partner.

1. Which parts of the lecture were easy for you to retell? Put a plus (+) by the easy parts. Put a minus (–) by the difficult parts. Tell why they were easy or difficult to retell.

   _____ Part 1 Introduction and overview

   _____ Part 2 Physiological description of laughter

   _____ Part 3 Sociological effects of laughter

   _____ Part 4 Medical effects of laughter

   _____ Part 5 Psychological effects of laughter

2. Which kind of information was easier for you to retell? Put a plus (+) by the easy parts. Put a minus (–) by the difficult parts. Tell why.

   _____ The general ideas

   _____ The examples and details

3. In what ways did you and your partners help each other retell the information accurately? Put a check (✓) by all the statements that are true.

   _____ I told my partners the missing or incorrect information that I read in my exercises on questions, answers, numbers, and keywords.

   _____ I told my partners the missing or incorrect information that I recalled from my memory.

   _____ I gave my partners hints about the missing or incorrect information that I read in my notes.

   _____ I gave my partners hints about the missing or incorrect information that I recalled from my memory.

   _____ I asked my partners questions about the missing or incorrect information.

   _____ My partners retold everything perfectly. I did not need to help any of my partners.

   _____ I retold everything perfectly. My partners did not need to help me.

Tag Questions

In conversation, speakers often ask each other questions. One type of question is the tag question. A tag question is formed by adding a *tag* to a statement.

> Music has the power to entertain listeners, <u>doesn't it</u>?
> The United States is part of North America, <u>isn't it</u>?
> Most people don't get enough sleep, <u>do they</u>?

ACTIVITY 20 **Understanding tag questions**

    A tag question is added to a statement when a speaker wants confirmation or agreement from the listener. During lectures, instructors use tag questions to involve students in the topic.

Listen to these sentences from the lecture. Fill in the tag question you hear. The first one is done for you.

Statement	Tag
1. (No laughing allowed. I mean, totally, no more laughing.) You can't do that, _can you?_	doesn't it?
2. (Does laughing make you feel good or bad?) Generally it makes you feel good, great, happy, _____	can you?
3. If it's successful, the humorous joke or action makes you laugh, _____	doesn't it?
4. You've seen people cry when they laugh, _____	do you?
5. You never hear anyone laugh "ha-ho-ha-ho", _____	haven't you?
6. We don't all laugh at the same things, _____	do we?

Statement	Tag
7. Maybe you like to watch a certain comedy, but it isn't funny to your mother, _____	do you?
8. You laugh when you feel comfortable with people, _____	don't you?
9. You don't laugh much when you are all by yourself, _____	doesn't it?
10. Generally it makes you feel good, great, happy, _____	is it?

Examine the sentences in the chart above. Circle the verb in each statement above and the verb in the tag. For example,

You (can't do) that, (can) you?

Afterwards, complete the following sentences by underlining the correct word in each pair.

11. The tag consists of (one word / two words).

12. In the tag, the subject comes (before / after) the verb.

13. In the tag, the subject is a (noun / pronoun).

14. When the statement is positive, the verb in the tag is (positive / negative).

15. When the statement is negative, the verb in the tag is (positive / negative).

16. The verb in the statement and the verb in the tag are (the same tense / different tenses).

17. In the tag, the pronoun matches the (subject / object) in number.

18. When the verb in the statement is not a form of *TO BE*, the verb in the tag is (a main verb / an auxiliary verb).

19. In the tag, the stress is on the (verb / subject).

20. Tag questions are more common in (spoken / written) English.

ACTIVITY 21   **Using falling intonation on tag questions**

English speakers use tag questions to maintain the flow of conversation. A tag question starts with a statement and ends with a tag. If the speaker thinks the statement is true, the tag is spoken with falling intonation.

We don't all laugh at the same things, do we?

Listen to the falling intonation in these tag questions. Practice saying them. Use falling intonation on the tag.

⬜ Tags with *Is, Isn't, Are, Aren't*

1. Laughter is not the same as humor, is it?
2. Robin Williams isn't a doctor, is he?
3. Laughter is a great thing, isn't it?
4. Bill Cosby is a famous comedian, isn't he?
5. You aren't sleeping, are you?
6. You are my partner, aren't you?
7. There are laughter clubs all over the world, aren't there?

⬜ Tags with *Do, Don't, Does, Doesn't*

1. People don't laugh when they're alone, do they?
2. You don't usually think of stress as positive, do you?
3. You laugh when someone tickles you, don't you?
4. Laughter doesn't cost anything, does it?
5. Your mother doesn't laugh at everything you do, does she?
6. Laughter has many benefits, doesn't it?
7. Comfortable means relaxed and restful, doesn't it?

⬜ Making tag questions

Listen carefully. Your instructor will say a sentence. Retell the same idea using a tag question. Use falling intonation on the tag. Try not to look at the book.

Example 1
Instructor: I think laughter is a great thing.
Student: Laughter is a great thing, isn't it?

Example 2
Instructor: Laughter is certainly not the same thing as humor.
Student: Laughter is not the same as humor, is it?

ACTIVITY 22   Answering tag questions

When you answer a tag question, use No *with a negative verb. Use* Yes *with a positive verb.*

Tag Question	Expected Answer
You're my partner, aren't you?	Yes, I am.
Laughter is not the same as humor, is it?	No, it isn't.

Go back to Activity 21. With a partner, practice asking and answering the tag questions.

 ACTIVITY 23   Listening for tag questions in dialogues

In casual conversation, people have different ways to say *Yes* and *No*.

We don't have any homework tonight, do we?

Possible Answers

Yes.	No.
Yeah.	Nope.
Yep.	Uh-uh.
Uh-huh.	Mm-mm.
Mm-hmm.	(Shake your head from side to side.)
(Nod your head up and down.)	

Listen to the dialogues without looking at the written words. Listen for the meaning, the falling intonation on the tag question, and the answers. Who's talking? What are they talking about? Jot down the topic and the speakers. Discuss the dialogues with the class.

Topic	Speakers	
1. homework	A: student	B: student (classmate)
2.	A:	B:
3.	A:	B:
4.	A:	B:
5.	A:	B:

Practice the dialogues with a partner. Nod or shake your head. Use falling intonation on the tag.

1. **A:** We don't have any homework tonight, <u>do we</u>?

   B: Nope. The teacher is giving us a break.

   A: We're lucky.

2. **A:** You're ready to give your speech today, aren't you?

   B: Yes, professor. I'm ready.

   A: That's good.

3. **A:** Your major is sociology, isn't it?

   B: Yes, ma'am. I want to be a sociologist. Can you tell me which courses to take?

   A: Sure. Let's look at the list of requirements.

4. **A:** Oh no, it's eight o'clock. The library isn't open now, is it?

   B: Uh-uh. It closes at seven on Fridays.

   A: I guess I'll have to come back tomorrow.

5. **A:** You know who Robin Williams is, don't you?

   B: Of course. My favorite movie is Mrs. Doubtfire.

   A: Really? It's mine too!

   B: You don't have that on DVD, do you?

   A: Uh-uh. But I have it on videotape.

   B: Let's watch it again!

ACTIVITY 24 Using transitions: *I mean, that is, in other words*

That is and *in other words* are used in both speaking and writing. *I mean* is less formal. You will hear it in conversation. Speakers usually pause slightly after a transition.

With a partner, practice making sentences. Start with the information in the left column. Choose a transition phrase. Finish with the paraphrase or explanation in the right column. Take turns. When it is your turn to speak, try to look at your partners. When it is your turn to listen, help your speaking partner with pronunciation, stress, and intonation.

Information	Transition	Paraphrase/Explanation
People laugh at a lot of things.	I mean,	things that are funny, silly, or foolish.
Laughter consists of two parts.		a set of gestures and a sound.
Laughter spasms start down here. When one friend laughs, the other one laughs,too.		between the abdomen and the lungs.
We usually think of stress as negative.	In other words,	being stressed, tense, upset, or worried.
Laughing makes you breathe more deeply.		it gives your lungs a good workout.
The more you laugh, the more active your T-cells become.		laughter stimulates the immune system.
Laughter is contagious.		when you laugh, others around you laugh too.
The basic form of laughter consists of repeated vowel-like notes.	That is,	"ha-ha-ha" or "ho-ho-ho" but not "ha-ho-ha-ho."

ACTIVITY 25 **Watching a silent comedy**

Movies change in popularity over time. Humor changes, too. However, some comedies have remained popular for many generations. Among the classic comedies are the works of Charlie Chaplin, Abbot and Costello, W.C. Fields, Buster Keaton, and the Marx Brothers. These comedians started acting before films had sound, so their early works were silent movies or radio shows. Silent movies depend a great deal on gestures, facial expressions, situations, and pranks.[7]

The Marx Brothers—Harpo, Groucho, Zeppo, and Chico—in *The Cocoanuts*, 1929

Charlie Chaplin in the role of The Little Tramp in *Modern Times*, 1936

Your instructor will show part of a silent movie in class or ask you to watch one outside of class. After watching about fifteen minutes, stop the movie.

In groups, discuss what you saw (people, things, actions, gestures, facial expressions, pranks). What made you laugh? Ask and answer questions about what you thought was funny.

Useful Language

Q. What (do you think) was funny?
A. [noun/noun phrase] was/were funny.

Ex. Groucho's eyebrows and facial expressions were funny.

Q. What did you laugh at? When did you laugh?
A. When [subject] [verb], I laughed (a little/very hard).

Ex. When the Tramp got caught in the machine, I laughed very hard.

7. *prank* (*n.*) = a mischievous trick or silly joke done for fun and amusement

ACTIVITY 26 Watching a talking comedy

I Love Lucy

After some boys took away the ladder from the bunk bed, Lucy tried to get into the top bunk by using stilts.

When television began, Lucille Ball's comedy show the *I Love Lucy Show*, was a huge success. During its broadcast from 1951 to 1957, this show was the number one rated TV show for four years: 67.3 percent of all American households with TVs were watching her show. Nowadays, reruns[8] are still shown on television.

Your instructor will show part of a talking comedy in class or ask you to watch one outside of class. After watching about fifteen minutes, stop the movie.

In groups, discuss what you saw (people, things, actions, gestures, facial expressions, pranks). Also discuss what you heard. What made you laugh? Discuss what you thought was funny. Ask your instructor questions about language, especially idioms and slang, that are new to you.

8. *rerun* (*n.*) = a repeat showing of recorded entertainment, especially a TV series

ACTIVITY 27 Preparing a report on a comedy

With your class, make a list of comedy movies and shows in English that you can recommend to your classmates. Put a check in the appropriate column: television sitcom, movie that is currently playing in a nearby movie theater, or movie that is currently available on videotape or DVD in a library or rental shop.

Title of movie or show	TV sitcom	Movie theater	DVD/ video
1.			
2.			
3.			
4.			
5.			
6.			
7.			
8.			
9.			
10.			
11.			
12.			
13.			
14.			
15.			
16.			

Choose a movie or TV sitcom that you think will be humorous. If you can watch it on videotape or DVD, you will be able to review parts of it as many times as you like. Write a one-page report. In your report, include the following information:

Characters: Describe two or three of the main characters (names, relationship, occupations).

Story: Briefly describe what happened. (What problems did the characters encounter? How did they resolve them?)

Humor: Describe what made you laugh (situations, interactions, pranks, language, gestures).

ACTIVITY 28 Presenting a report on a comedy

Speaker

Give a two-minute speech to introduce the comedy you selected in Activity 27. Your instructor will let you know if you may use your written report as a guide. When you are speaking, try to use one or two transitions as in Activity 24. If possible, bring a video recording (tape or disc) of your show. After your report, show a one-minute clip of a humorous part of the show.

Listeners

When you are listening to a partner's presentation, repeat key information for confirmation and clarification. Ask questions about meaning (Ch. 4 Activity 22) and ask questions about differences (Ch. 4 Activity 23). Take brief notes in your notebook using a chart like the one below.

Speaker # Name
Title of comedy
Characters
Story
Humor
Other interesting points

ACTIVITY 29 Reading riddles and jokes

Read the following riddles and jokes and discuss them with your class.

Riddles

1. Why are fish so smart?   Because they live in schools.

2. What pool is no good for swimming?   A car pool.

3. What word begins with E, ends
   with E, and sounds as if it has only
   one letter in it?   Eye (I).

4. Why is B such a hot letter?   Because it makes oil boil.

5. How did the ocean say good-bye?   It waved.

Jokes

1. The Japanese eat little fat and suffer fewer heart attacks than the British or Americans.

   The French eat a lot of fat and also suffer fewer heart attacks than the British or Americans.

   The Italians drink a lot of red wine and also suffer fewer heart attacks than the British or Americans.

   Conclusion: Eat and drink what you like. Speaking English is apparently what kills you.

   *   *   *

2. Two elderly ladies had been friends for many decades. Over the years they had shared all kinds of activities and adventures. Lately, their activities had been limited to meeting a few times a week to play cards.
   One day they were playing cards when one looked at the other and said, "Now don't get mad at me, I know we've been friends for a long time, but I just can't think of your name! I've thought and thought, but I can't remember it. Please tell me what your name is."
   Her friend glared at her. For at least three minutes she just stared and glared at her.
   Finally she said, "How soon do you need to know?"

Do you know any riddles or jokes? If you do, share them with your classmates.

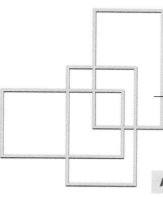

Part 3

ACTIVITY 30 Applying information and skills

Your instructor may ask you to write down the answers to the questions, discuss these questions in a group, and/or record your oral answers to the questions.

1. Describe two physiological characteristics of laughter.

   _____

   _____

   _____

2. Describe two sociological characteristics of laughter.

   _____

   _____

   _____

3. Describe two medical effects of laughter.

   _____

   _____

   _____

4. Describe two psychological effects of laughter.

   _____

   _____

   _____

5. Is laughter important in your life? Explain.

   _____

   _____

   _____

6. Complete the sentences a–d about tag questions.

   a. When the statement is positive, the verb in the tag is _____.

   b. When the statement is negative, the verb in the tag is _____.

   c. In the tag, the stress is on the _____.

   d. If the speaker thinks the statement is true, the tag is spoken with _____ intonation.

7. Add tags to sentences a–g.

   a. Laughter is good for you, _____?

   b. People don't laugh much by themselves, _____?

   c. You sometimes laugh when you see other people laughing, _____?

   d. She laughs when someone tickles her, _____?

   e. Your major is psychology, _____?

   f. He doesn't want to get sick, _____?

   g. We don't have a test today, _____?

8. Combine a sentence from the first column with a phrase from the last column. Use a transition to connect them.

Information	Transition	Paraphrase/Explanation
Some scientists approach laughter from a physiological point of view.	I mean,	totally, no more laughing.
Other researchers approach it from a psychological point of view.		they show how laughter affects a person's illness and health.
Still others approach this topic from a sociological viewpoint.	In other words,	we can't perceive anything around us.
People in the health profession approach laughter from a medical viewpoint.		they examine how laughter works in social interactions.
How many meals will you have consumed in your lifetime?	That is,	it nourishes or promotes growth.
No laughing allowed.		altogether in your whole life?
A nutrient is an ingredient in your diet that has nutritious qualities.	What I mean to say is,	geography is the study of land and people.
Geography is more than the study of the land.		the way laughter affects your mind and your emotions.
Sleep is a state of complete perceptual disengagement from the environment.	That means	the way your body functions to make laughter.

ACTIVITY **31** **Reviewing pronunciation, stress, and fluency**

Review these words and sentences with a partner. Pronounce each item as clearly and fluently as you can. Have your partner listen and help you with your pronunciation of syllables, stress, and intonation. Take turns. Your instructor may ask you to record your pronunciation of these items and others in this chapter.

1. approaches   [_3_ - _2_]   7. variation   [___ - ___]

2. benefit   [___ - ___]   8. positive   [___ - ___]

3. comfortable   [___ - ___]   9. vibrate   [___ - ___]

4. design   [___ - ___]   10. medical   [___ - ___]

5. individual   [___ - ___]   11. survive   [___ - ___]

6. role   [___ - ___]   12. sociology   [___ - ___]

Use falling intonation on the tag quesiton.

13. **A:** Leslie is very efficient in her profession, isn't she?
    B: Yes. She performs her job very confidently.

14. **A:** Laughter has many benefits, doesn't it?
    B: Yes. Let's examine the connection between laughter and health.

15. **A:** Your major isn't psychology, is it?
    B: No, it isn't. It's physiology.

ACTIVITY 32 **Taking dictation**

In this dictation, you will hear vocabulary and sentence patterns that you practiced in this chapter. Your instructor will tell you the number of words in each sentence. Write the numbers within the parentheses and use them as a guide. You will hear each sentence three times. First, listen and try to understand the meaning of the whole sentence. Second, listen and write. Third, listen and check.

1. _____ (_____ words)
   _____

2. _____ (_____ words)
   _____

3. _____ (_____ words)
   _____

4. _____ (_____ words)
   _____

5. _____ (_____ words)
   _____

6. _____ (_____ words)
   _____

7. _____ (_____ words)
   _____

8. _____ (_____ words)
   _____

9. _____ (_____ words)
   _____

10. _____ (_____ words)
    _____

ACTIVITY 33   Summarizing and checking your progress

How well can you perform the following objectives?

I can . . .	Barely	Somewhat	Fairly well	Very well
Use vocabulary and expressions to discuss laughter.				
Use a dictionary to learn the pronunciation of new words.				
Pronounce academic vocabulary with proper syllables and stress.				
Identify and use transitions for introducing a paraphrase or an explanation: *in other words, that is, I mean.*				
Recognize the relationship between main ideas and examples.				
Ask tag questions with falling intonation.				
Talk about the humorous elements of a comedy.				
Relate the contents of the lecture to laughter in my own life.				
Take dictation of sentences related to laughter.				

WEB POWER

You will find additional exercises related to the content in this chapter at http://esl.college.hmco.com/students.

Google: A Business Dream Come True

ACADEMIC FOCUS: GENERAL BUSINESS
▶ BUSINESS AND TECHNOLOGY

Academic Listening and Speaking Objectives

In this chapter, you will continue to develop your skills as an academic listener and speaker. You will hear a lecture that an instructor gives in a general business course. You will learn to pronounce academic vocabulary, and you will practice discussing topics related to business and technology. You will participate in listening, speaking, and thinking activities. In particular, you will:

- **Develop vocabulary and expressions to discuss business and technology**
- **Use a dictionary to learn the pronunciation of new academic words**
- **Hear, identify, and pronounce key vocabulary with proper syllables and word stress**
- **Use a case study as a learning tool**
- **Apply general concepts of business to a specific case**
- **Learn the meanings, form, stress, and linking patterns of new phrasal verbs**
- **Hear, identify, and pronounce -ed endings /t/, /d/, and /ɪd/**
- **Understand and use tag questions with rising intonation**
- **Ask questions using regular and irregular past tense forms**
- **Ask and answer questions about business and technology**
- **Relate the contents of the lecture to personal use of technology**
- **Take dictation of sentences related to business and technology**

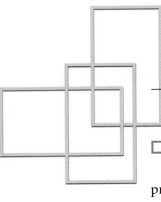

Part 1

☐ Getting Ready for the Lecture

Business refers to the activities of people buying and selling products. Business also refers to an organization of people, buildings, and products or services, in other words, a commercial enterprise. When you study business, you learn about the nature of business and about types of business organization.

ACTIVITY 1 Engaging in business

In a small group of three or four students, look at the illustrations. Describe each picture and take notes. Discuss the questions with your partners.

What kind of business is shown? Who is the customer? What kinds of products are available at this business? Is the customer buying goods (things) or services? How is the salesperson selling the product? How is the customer choosing the product to buy?

A.	Business
	Customer(s)
	Product(s)
	Sales method
	Buying method
B.	Business
	Customer(s)
	Product(s)
	Sales method
	Buying method

C.	Business
	Customer(s)
	Product(s)
	Sales method
	Buying method

D.	Business
	Customer(s)
	Product(s)
	Sales method
	Buying method

E.	Business
	Customer(s)
	Product(s)
	Sales method
	Buying method

F.	Business
	Customer(s)
	Product(s)
	Sales method
	Buying method

Do you engage in business like the ones shown in the pictures? As a businessperson or as a customer?

🔲 **Looking at Language**

🎧   **ACTIVITY 2**   **Identifying syllables and word stress**

Listen to the pronunciation of these words. Clap or tap the number of syllables you hear. Then write the syllable-stress code. The first one is done for you.

1. commercial (*adj.*)   [_3_ - _2_]

2. experiment (*intr.v.*)   [___ - ___]

3. query (*n.*)   [___ - ___]

4. graduate (*n.*)   [___ - ___]

5. reward (*tr.v.*)   [___ - ___]

6. advertising (*n.*)   [___ - ___]

7. information (*n.*)   [___ - ___]

8. risk (*tr.v.*)   [___ - ___]

9. business (*n.*)   [___ - ___]

10. Internet (*n.*)   [___ - ___]

11. search (*tr.v., intr.v.*)   [___ - ___]

12. catalog (*n.*)   [___ - ___]

13. profit (*n.*)   [___ - ___]

14. customer, (*n.*)   [___ - ___]

After you mark the syllable-stress code, take turns saying the words to your partner. Pronounce each word with the correct number of syllables. Make the stressed syllable long, strong, and high. Hear and feel the beats by clapping as you pronounce. Help your partner pronounce the words with correct syllables and stress.

ACTIVITY **3** **Taking dictation**

You will hear the words above in context. You will hear each sentence three times. First, listen and try to understand the meaning of the whole sentence. Second, listen and write. Third, listen and check. Use the number of words in the parentheses as a guide.

1. _____ (12 words)

   _____

2. _____ (12 words)

   _____

3. _____ (14 words)

   _____

4. _____ (13 words)

   _____

5. _____ (9 words)

   _____

6. _____ (11 words)

   _____

7. _____ (7 words)

   _____

8. _____ (10 words)

   _____

9. _____ (9 words)

   _____

ACTIVITY 4 **Matching words with definitions**

Write a word from the list next to its definition.

advertising (*n.*)   commercial (*adj.*)   graduate (*n.*)
profit (*n.*)   risk (*tr.v.*)   business (*n.*)
customer (*n.*)   information (*n.*)   query (*n.*)
search (*tr.v., intr.v.*)   catalog (*n.*)   experiment (*intr.v.*)
Internet (*n.*)   reward (*tr.v.*)

1. _____ An enterprise of people buying and selling products.

2. _____ To try sthg. new, especially in order to gain experience.

3. _____ The field of making print, radio, or TV descriptions to promote products and services.

4. _____ Knowledge, news, facts, especially about a certain event or subject.

5. _____ A huge computer network of electronic mail and information on computers, used by millions of people and organizations all over the world. Used with *the*.

6. _____ To put (sbdy./sthg.) in a situation where there is a chance of harm or loss.

7. _____ To make a careful examination of (sthg.) in order to find sthg. or sbdy.

8. _____ A person or business that buys goods or services.

9. _____ A booklet containing information about products, school courses, etc.

10. _____ A person who has received an academic degree or diploma.

11. _____ To give money, a bonus, or a prize to sbdy. in return for good behavior or a special service.

12. _____ A question; an inquiry; a request for information.

13. _____ Relating to business; engaged in commerce.

14. _____ The money made in a business investment.

ACTIVITY 5   **Learning the vocabulary of academic lectures**

Look up each academic word in an English dictionary. Copy the pronunciation of each word exactly. Use the part of speech to guide you to the right entry. Write the syllable-stress code. Study the definition. Then compare your answers with a classmate's. The first one is done for you.

1. analysis
   (*n.*)   <u>a•nal•y•sis</u>   <u>ə-năl'ĭ-sĭs</u>   [<u>4</u> - <u>2</u>]

   The separation of sthg. into its parts in order to determine its nature.

2. available
   (*adj.*)   ————————   ————————   [—— - ——]

   Willing or able to serve; capable of being obtained.

3. computer
   (*n.*)   ————————   ————————   [—— - ——]

   An electronic device that stores and processes information according to a set of instructions (programs) stored within the device.

4. constitute
   (*tr.v.*)   ————————   ————————   [—— - ——]

   To be the elements or parts of sthg.; compose.

5. credit
   (*n.*)   ————————   ————————   [—— - ——]

   Recognition, praise, points, etc. for an act, ability, or quality.

6. distinction
   (*n.*)   ————————   ————————   [—— - ——]

   The condition or fact of being different and separate; a clear difference.

7. equation
   (*n.*)   ————————   ————————   [—— - ——]

   A mathematical statement that two amounts are equal.

8. establish
   (*tr.v.*)   ————————   ————————   [—— - ——]

   To create, set up, found (a company, school, etc.).

9. funding
   (*n.*)   ————————   ————————   [—— - ——]

   Financial support; money provided for a specific purpose.

10. income
    (*n.*)   ————————   ————————   [—— - ——]

    Money earned from working or from the sale of goods, property, or investments.

11. incorporate
    (*intr.v.*)
    _____   _____   [___ - ___]

    To form a corporation, a company recognized by
    law as a single body with its own powers separate
    from its individual members.

12. invest
    (*tr.v.*)
    _____   _____   [___ - ___]

    To put (money) into sthg. in order to earn interest
    or make a profit.

13. link
    (*n.*)
    _____   _____   [___ - ___]

    Something that connects things in a series, such as a
    ring in a chain, or stations in a communication
    system.

14. purchase
    (*tr.v.*)
    _____   _____   [___ - ___]

    To buy (sthg.), to get goods and services in
    exchange for money.

15. relevant
    (*adj.*)
    _____   _____   [___ - ___]

    Closely connected, appropriate.

16. revenue
    (*n.*)
    _____   _____   [___ - ___]

    Money that comes into a business from the sale of
    goods or services.

17. secure
    (*vt.*)
    _____   _____   [___ - ___]

    (formal) To obtain.

18. site
    (*n.*)
    _____   _____   [___ - ___]

    An area or place; a web site.

19. technology
    (*n.*)
    _____   _____   [___ - ___]

    Science used in practical applications, especially in
    industry and commerce.

ACTIVITY 6   Checking and pronouncing the vocabulary

*Listen to the pronunciation of each word in the previous activity. Check the
syllable-stress code.*

*Pronounce each word with your instructor or the recording, and then
practice with a partner.*

ACTIVITY 7 Listening to academic vocabulary in context

Listen to the sentences and complete each one with a word from the academic word list in the previous activity. Sometimes you will hear different forms of the words on the list. Write the form that you hear.

1. $3 \times 2 = 6$ is a simple _____.

2. A _____ can do a mathematical _____ very quickly.

3. He got _____ to the computer lab by showing his identity card.

4. Keyboarding and word processing are _____ skills in any academic field.

5. The professor is _____ to see you in her office from 1:00 to 2:30.

6. The instructor gave the students _____ for each assignment they handed in.

7. There is a _____ between distance learning and face-to-face classes.

8. She _____ a book and CD for her English class.

9. Advances in _____ have improved the standard of living.

10. On this webpage, clicking on the _____ "top" will take you to the beginning of the page.

11. Business is a commercial or industrial enterprise and the people who

     _____ it.

12. Start-up companies try to get _____ from investors who
    are interested in their product.

13. When he got a job promotion, he had more responsibilities and a
    higher _____.

14. He _____ his savings in stocks and bonds.

15. The entrepreneurs _____ funding for their business from
    several investors.

16. They _____ a corporation to import products from China.

17. They built a new warehouse on the _____ of an old farm.

18. They _____ their business in the state of California.

19. They expect their business _____ to increase by $50,000 in
    two years.

POWER GRAMMAR

Verbs That End in -ed

The past tense is used to describe conditions and actions that
occurred in the past. In the lecture, you will hear many instances of the
past tense. Regular past tense verbs are composed of the base form of
a verb and an -ed ending. For example:

> We <u>discussed</u> a few examples.
> They <u>majored</u> in computer science.
> They <u>started</u> a company.

ACTIVITY **8**   Listening to verbs with *-ed* endings

> In spoken English, the *-ed* ending is pronounced in three distinct ways:
> /t/, /d/, and /ɪd/. You can hear those ways in the pronunciation of
> <u>discussed</u>, <u>majored</u>, and <u>started</u>.

*Listen to the base form and -ed forms[1] of the following verbs. You will hear
the -ed forms of these verbs in the lecture.*

/t/		/d/		/ɪd/	
ask	asked	show	showed	note	noted
look	looked	study	studied	start	started
like	liked	worry	worried	count	counted
hook	hooked	call	called	want	wanted
rank	ranked	handle	handled	insist	insisted
stop	stopped	form	formed	request	requested
develop	developed	name	named	create	created
surf	surfed	define	defined	invest	invested
laugh	laughed	explain	explained	include	included
base	based	hire	hired	found	founded
discuss	discussed	secure	secured	decide	decided
increase	increased	consider	considered	need	needed
purchase	purchased	believe	believed	expand	expanded
force	forced	use	used	add	added
cash	cashed	analyze	analyzed	provide	provided
search	searched	encourage	encouraged	succeed	succeeded

Complete the sentences about the sound of the regular past tense.

1. If the base form ends with the sound /t/ or /d/, pronounce the *-ed* as _____ .	**a.** the single voiceless sound /t/
2. If the base form ends with a voiceless sound except /t/, pronounce the *-ed* as _____ .	**b.** the single voiced sound /d/
3. If the base form ends with a voiced sound except /d/, pronounce the *-ed* as _____ .	**c.** the extra syllable /ɪd/

1. *-ed* ending are also used for past participle verb forms and adjectives, e.g.,
tired, excited.

ACTIVITY 9   Distinguishing between verb forms

Listen to the sentences. Underline the present or past verb form you hear in each sentence.

1. I (ask / asked) you about your company.

2. We (want / wanted) to know about your business.

3. They (need / needed) to secure funding for their enterprise.

4. The teachers (explain / explained) all of the words.

5. I (surf / surfed) on the Internet.

6. We (laugh / laughed) at the funny jokes.

7. I (encourage / encouraged) her to complete her college education.

8. They (develop / developed) a new product.

9. We (discuss / discussed) the business plan.

10. I (succeed / succeeded) in securing a business loan.

POWER GRAMMAR

Irregular Past Tense Verbs

Some verbs have irregular past forms. They do not end in *-ed*. For example:

> Did the company grow?
> Yes, the company grew fast.

> Did two companies become partners?
> Yes, Google and Yahoo became technology partners.

> Where did you go?
> I went to my business class.

ACTIVITY 10   Listening to irregular past tense verbs

In this lecture, you will hear irregular past tense verbs like the ones below. These past tense forms do not have -*ed* endings.

Work with a partner. Write the past tense verb forms in the blanks. Then listen to the sentences.

		Base Form	Past Tense
1.	I _went_ to my classroom. I _____ a test. I _____ close attention to the directions. The test _____ quite easy. I _____ the main ideas. I _____ the answers carefully. The instructor _____ me full credit for my responses. I said, "Great!" I _____ home very satisfied.	be come get give pay say take write	was, were came got gave paid said took wrote
2.	Eric and Sue _____ an idea for a new medical device. They _____ about it for a long time. They _____ with investors. The investors _____ their plan. They all _____ partners. They _____ a company name.	become choose have hear meet think	became chose had heard met thought
3.	Daniel and his business partners _____ some important decisions. They _____ an oil refinery. They _____ a hundred wells in the oil field. They _____ oil back to the refinery. Their company _____ fast. They _____ a lot of oil products. Before long, they _____ very rich.	bring build feel grow make sell	brought built felt grew made sold

⬭ Getting Information from the Lecture

This lecture in a business class begins with a review of a test. It continues with a case study of the company called Google. You will listen to each part of the lecture several times. Each time you will listen for a specific purpose. Later you will listen to the whole lecture.

ACTIVITY 11 Going over a test

When instructors hand back tests to students, they often make remarks about the content of the test and the students' answers.

Follow the text as your instructor reads the sentences below. Listen to the first half of the lecture. Circle each of the actions the lecturer took after handing back the tests to the class. Afterwards, discuss your answers with the class.

Master Student Tip

When an instructor reviews test items, listen carefully. This is another opportunity to learn. If there are parts you don't understand clearly, be sure to ask questions.

The Instructor. . .

1. (told / didn't tell) the answers to every test item.

2. (told / didn't tell) students where to find the answers to the test questions.

3. (explained / didn't explain) correct responses.

4. (explained / didn't explain) why some responses are incorrect.

5. (shared / didn't share) student responses to some test items.

6. (gave / didn't give) information about grades or points.

7. (told / didn't tell) how the test items relate to other learning activities.

8. (emphasized / didn't emphasize) information that will be on another test.

9. (praised / didn't praise) students for their good work.

10. (warned / didn't warn) students to study harder.

11. (invited / didn't invite) students to ask questions about the test now.

12. (invited / didn't invite) students to come to office hours with their questions.

ACTIVITY 12 **Listening for key terms**

In the first half of the lecture, you hear the definitions of six key business terms. You will take notes about these six terms in the chart on the next pages.

First, preview the sentences in the left column and word choices in the right column. Listen to your instructor pronounce the words. Keep the words in your auditory memory.

Next, listen to the first half of the lecture again. As you listen this time, listen for the definitions of key terms and examples. Complete each group of sentences with the words from the box on the right. You will use most of the word choices to complete the sentences. You will not use all of the words. You will use some words twice. The, circle a *or* an, *which ever is correct. Finally, write the key term above the group of sentences. An example has been done for you.*

1. Key term: _Business_	business businessperson commercial constitute customers profit ✓
Definition: Business is enterprise that, for ⓐ/ an _profit_ provides value-creating products for _____. Business is a / an or industrial enterprise and the people who _____ it.	
2. Key term: _____	enterprise entrepreneur French make money risks
Definition: An entrepreneur is a person who takes on a / an _____. This businessperson _____ her or his time and money to take on an enterprise. The _____ tries to _____ doing so.	

3. Key term: _____

   Definition: Products are _____ goods or _____.

   Examples: An example of a physical good is a / an _____. An

   example of a service is a / an _____. An example

   of a _____ that is both a good and a service is

   a / an _____.

   | cell phone |
   | computer |
   | Internet service provider |
   | physical |
   | product |
   | services |
   | telephone |

4. Key term: _____

   Definition: _____ are the people who buy a business's products.

   Customers _____ a company's _____

   or _____.

   | customers |
   | goods |
   | purchase |
   | sell |
   | services |

5. Key term: _____

   Definition: Creating value means giving _____ their money's worth;

   that is, giving them _____ than they can make or more than they

   can _____ themselves for the same amount of money and

   _____. Example: You are willing to fill up your car at a / an

   _____. The oil company oil field _____

   for your money.

   | customers |
   | created value |
   | creating value |
   | do |
   | gas station |
   | more |
   | oil field |
   | time |

6. Key term: _____

   A profit is a _____, or return, on a business _____.

   _____ means getting more money back from your enterprise

   than you _____ on it.

   Equation: Profit = _____ — _____

   | expenses |
   | gain |
   | investment |
   | loss |
   | profit |
   | sales revenue |
   | spend |

ACTIVITY 13   Lecture Part 1: Reviewing key terms

Besides the key business terms, the lecturer gives information about other aspects of business.

Listen to the first half of the lecture again. Write short answers to the following questions. You may use some phrases from the box in your answers.

¹⁄₂, ¹⁄₂	make a profit	case studies	makes a loss
now in class	shut down	later during office hours	

1. What happens if the business does not make a profit—the expenses are more than sales revenue?

   _____

   _____

2. How many businesses succeed, and how many fail?

   _____

   _____

3. Why do entrepreneurs do business?

   _____

   _____

4. If students have questions about the test, when and where can they ask them?

   _____

   _____

5. What does the lecturer want to discuss now?

   _____

   _____

ACTIVITY 14 Listening for main ideas

The lecture continues with a case study of the company called Google. When you listen to this part of the lecture for the first time, try to get an overview. Don't worry about understanding everything. You will have a chance to listen to it again.

Preview the sentences below. Then listen to Part 2 of the lecture for the first time. Underline all of the phrases that apply (one or more).

1. Google is used (to search the Internet for information / instead of a library).

2. To use Google, you need (a computer / Internet access / an encyclopedia and a news archive).

3. Google was founded by two Stanford (mathematics professors / computer science graduate students / Russian students).

4. The founders of the company recognized that finding information was (really important / a very big problem for the world / impossible).

5. Google's search technology was (the same as / different from) earlier search engines.

6. Larry Page and Sergey Brin needed (a drawer / investors / a co-founder) to start their business.

7. Google started in (1995 / 1998 / 2000).

8. Google grew (very slowly / at a moderate rate / very fast).

9. Google earned money from (commercial clients / advertising / users).

10. In 2003, Google handled (10,000 / 200 million / 3 billion) search queries a day.

🎧   **ACTIVITY 15   Lecture Part 2: Listening for details**

When you listen to the story of Google again, you will be able to catch more details.

Preview the sentences below. Then listen to Part 2 of the lecture for the second time. Underline <u>all</u> of the phrases that apply.

1. The lecturer thinks everybody with a computer that's hooked up to the Internet (knew / knows / will know) how to do a basic search with Google.
2. (You have to pay a cent per search / It is free) to use Google.
3. The company is based in (California / Michigan / Moscow / Silicon Valley).
4. A (googol / google / googel) is a mathematical term for a one (1) followed by 100 zeros.
5. Larry Page and Sergey Brin (were / were not) the only graduate students to use Stanford as an experimental lab before starting a business.
6. Google's search engine (counted keywords in websites / analyzed the links among web pages).
7. The software that runs Google was named after (Larry Page / Sergey Brin / both / neither).
8. The founders realized that (no one / some people / everyone) in the world wanted information.
9. Investor Andy Bechtolsheim made out a check to Google, Inc. for a ($1,000 / $10,000 / $100,000 / $1,000,000).
10. He gave them the check (before / after) the company existed.
11. Larry Page and Sergey Brin established Google with the financial support from (Andy Bechtolsheim / family / friends).
12. In a few (weeks / months / years) *PC Magazine* named Google one of its Top 100 Web Sites and Search Engines for 1998.
13. Google's revenue comes from (newspaper ads / pop-up ads / small ads on the side of a webpage / companies that use its technology).

🎧 **ACTIVITY 16** **Listening for past tense**

Short passages from the lecture follow. These parts of the lecture use past tense and past participle verb forms.

With a partner, complete the sentences below with past tense and past participle verbs. Some are regular, and others are irregular. Use the list of base form verbs as a guide. The first sentence is done for you.

Afterwards, listen to the entire lecture for the third time. Check your answers.

1. I _asked_ you to define business. Most of you _defined_ it very well. You did not all define it in exactly the same words, but as long as you _got_ the main idea I _gave_ you credit for it.	ask define get give
2. I _____ you to explain two types of products, and then I _____ for two examples of each to show you know the distinction between the two. You _____ that products are physical goods—things—or services. Sometimes both. For physical goods, some of you _____ things like a computer, a banana, and a dress. For services, some of you _____ a movie show, a haircut, and an ISP—an Internet service provider. Somebody _____ that a cell phone is both a good and a service.	ask ask explain note request say write
3. You did not have to do all the work. Somebody else _____ a lot of really expensive machines, _____ to an oil field, dug a hole, looked for petroleum, _____ it back to a refinery, turned it into gasoline, _____ a gas station, _____ gas pumps, and all that.	bring build go install purchase

4. A couple of you even _____ the hook up equation in your answer: Profit equals sales revenue minus expenses.

hook up
include
search

5. How many of you search the Internet? Have you _____ it lately? Well, let me tell you, before long, I think everybody with a computer that's _____ to the Internet will be familiar with Google, at least know how to do a basic search with Google.

6. But not everyone knows the story of Google, that is, how it started, why it was _____, how it formed, and how it _____. Where is this company based? Anyone know? It's _____ in Silicon Valley, in Mountain View, California. So let's talk about when and how Google _____. Google was _____ by two Stanford graduate students, Larry Page and Sergey Brin.

base
create
develop
found
start

7. So they _____ their math skills to create a computer program. Their software _____ the links among hundreds and thousands of webpages. It _____ the webpages, from more relevant to less relevant. Their system _____ much better search results than the older search engines.

analyze
produce
rank
use

8. They _____ that finding information was really important, and a very big problem for the world. They decided they _____ to help people find information, and they _____ they could also make money. So they _____ to go into business.

decide
know
recognize
want

9. They quickly _____ more funding from other people—family and friends. After they _____ Google as a business, they _____ the check, all of the checks.

cash
establish
secure

10. So Google _____. And then they _____ more commercial clients. And they _____ many, many more awards, including *Time* magazine's Top Ten Best Cybertech list for 1999, and a Webby Award in May 2000. Shortly after that, they _____ another revenue source, and do you know what that was? Advertising.

add
expand
receive
sign on

▭ Using your Notes to Apply Information

ACTIVITY 17 Applying information to a case study

The lecture began with a discussion of key business terms. It continued with a case study of the company called Google. In this activity, you will apply the business terms to the case. Recall these sentences from the lecture:

> The entrepreneur creates value in a product. When a business creates value for customers, the customers reward the business by paying prices that make the business earn profits.

Refer to your notes in Activities 11–16. Write answers to the following questions. Then discuss them in groups of two or three classmates to improve your written answers.

1. Who is/are the entrepreneur(s) of this business? What is their background?

   _____

   _____

   _____

   _____

   _____

2. What product(s) does the company sell? Are they goods, services, or both?

   _____

   _____

   _____

   _____

   _____

3. Who uses the company's product(s)? Describe this company's customers.

_____

_____

_____

_____

_____

_____

4. In what way did this company create value for its customers? What does the company provide that the customer is willing to pay for?

_____

_____

_____

_____

_____

_____

5. Does the company make a profit? If so, how? If not, how does it plan to make a profit?

_____

_____

_____

_____

_____

_____

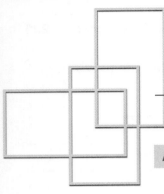

Part 2

ACTIVITY 18 Retelling the content of the lecture

STRATEGY

Retelling as a Comprehension Tool

Retelling helps you review and remember what you learned. When you retell, you recall information and think about the connections between main ideas and supporting details, between major and minor details. Naturally, retelling also benefits your classmates by giving them information that they missed.

Work in pairs to retell the information in the lecture. Look at your notes in Activities 11–17. Take turns retelling Parts 1 and 2 of the lecture. You do not need to remember the lecturer's exact words, but you must remember the ideas. Try to paraphrase these ideas. Speak in complete sentences. Use proper word stress (stress the right syllable in a word) and sentence stress (stress the keywords in a sentence). Pronounce s/es endings /s/, /z/, /ɪz/ and -ed endings, /t/, /d/, /ɪd/. Take turns as described below.

First retelling

Speaker A: Retell the first part of the lecture to your partner. Use your notes to remember the content.

Listener: Remind the speaker of missing points by giving some keywords or ideas.

Speaker B: Retell the second part of the lecture to your partner. Use your notes to remember the content.

Listener: Remind the speaker of missing points by giving some keywords or ideas.

Second retelling

Speaker A: Retell the first part of the lecture to your partner again. This time, try not to use your notes. Look at your listener.

Listener: Encourage and help the speaker with keywords or ideas.

Speaker B: Retell the second part of the lecture to your partner. This time, try not to use your notes. Look at your listener.

Listener: Encourage and help the speaker with keywords or ideas.

Switch roles so that each partner practices retelling part of the lecture.

Your instructor may call on you to retell part of the lecture to the whole class.

ACTIVITY 19   Checking how you retold the lecture

Answer the questions about yourself. Then discuss your answers with a partner.

1. How well did you retell the content of the lecture? Put a plus (+) by the easy part(s). Put a minus (–) by the difficult part(s). Tell why.

   _____ Part 1: Going over business terms from the test

   _____ Part 2: The story of Google

   _____ The main ideas

   _____ Details: key terms, definitions, and examples

2. How well did you express your ideas with good pronunciation? Put a plus (+) by the easy parts. Put a minus (–) by the difficult parts. Tell why.

   _____ I spoke in complete sentences.

   _____ Word stress: I stressed the correct syllable in words.

   _____ Sentence stress: I stressed the keyword in sentences.

   _____ Verbs with -*ed* endings: I pronounced /t/, /d/, and /ɪd/ accurately.

   _____ Nouns and verbs with *s/es* endings: I pronounced /s/, /z/, and /ɪz/ accurately.

3. In what ways did you and your partner help each other retell the information accurately and speak clearly? Put a check by all the statements that are true.

Myself	My partner
_____ I told my partner the missing or incorrect information.	_____ My partner told me the missing or incorrect information.
_____ I gave my partner hints about the missing or incorrect information that I read in my notes.	_____ My partner told me hints about the missing or incorrect information that I read in my notes.
_____ I asked my partner questions about the missing or incorrect information.	_____ My partner asked me questions about the missing or incorrect information.
_____ I corrected my partner's word stress.	_____ My partner corrected my word stress.
_____ I corrected my partner's sentence stress.	_____ My partner corrected my sentence stress.
_____ I corrected my partner's /t/, /d/, and /ɪd/ endings.	_____ My partner corrected my /t/, /d/, and /ɪd/ endings.
_____ I corrected my partner's /s/, /z/, and /ɪz/ endings.	_____ My partner corrected my /s/, /z/, and /ɪz/ endings.

ACTIVITY 20   Drawing conclusions

After you consider relevant facts, you often make a decision or form an opinion about something. This action is called *drawing a conclusion.*

In groups of three, discuss the following questions. Be prepared to report your group's conclusions to the class.

1. Do you think the founders' educational background had an influence on their business? If so, how did it affect their career choices?

_____

_____

_____

2. Do you need to be a computer programmer to search for information using a computer?

_____

_____

_____

3. How is Google like an encyclopedia, a phone book, a shopping catalog, and a news archive, all at once?

_____

_____

_____

4. How is searching for information on the Internet similar to searching for information in books and other printed materials? Different from it?

_____

_____

_____

5. Is Google the only search engine that you can use on the Internet?

_____

_____

_____

ACTIVITY 2 **Learning more phrasal verbs**

> In this lecture you heard phrasal verbs such as these:
>
> They <u>majored in</u> computer science.
> Articles about Google <u>showed up</u> in papers like *USA Today*.

Study the meanings of the phrasal verbs below. You heard them in the lecture. Then, using the past tense, complete the sentences.

Listen to the sentences. Pronounce them with good stress, intonation, and linking, as you learned in Chapter 4.[2]

Practice saying the sentences to a partner.

Separable Phrasal Verbs

1. **fill up** sthg. = to fill a gasoline tank in a car or truck

   We __*filled up*__ our car before we left on vacation.

   We _____ our car _____ before we left.

   We _____ it _____ at the gas station.

2. **hook up** sthg. = to connect

   He _____ _____ the TV and watched the news.

   He _____ the TV _____ and watched the news.

   He _____ it _____ and watched the news.

3. **look up** sthg. = to try to find sthg. in a dictionary or other reference book

   She _____ _____ the instructor's office hours on the

   information sheet.

   She _____ the instructor's office hours _____ on the

   information sheet.

   She _____ them _____ on the information sheet.

2. To review the form, stress, and intonation of phrasal verbs, see Chapter 4, Activities 6, 20, and 21.

4. **make out** sthg. = to write out; draw up

   I _____ _____ the invoices and faxed them

   to the customers.

   I _____ the invoices _____ and faxed them

   to the customers.

   I _____ them _____ and faxed them.

5. **set up** sthg. = to establish in business by providing capital, equipment, etc.

   You _____ _____ your company at a good time.

   You _____ your company _____ at a good time.

   You _____ it _____ at a good time.

6. **sign on** sbdy. = to engage by written agreement

   The company _____ _____ seven new customers.

   The company _____ seven new customers _____.

   The company _____ them _____.

7. **take on** sthg. = to undertake or begin to handle

   We all _____ _____ extra responsibilities willingly.

   We all _____ extra responsibilities _____ willingly.

   We all _____ them _____ willingly.

8. **think up** sthg. = to invent, to devise

   The employees _____ _____ interesting new ideas.

   The employees _____ interesting new ideas _____.

   The employees _____ them _____.

Inseparable Phrasal Verbs

9. **go into** sthg. = to enter a profession

   He _____ _____ business with his classmate.

   He _____ _____ business with him.

10. **go on with/to** sthg. = to continue

    The instructor finished Part 1 and _____ _____

    to Part 2.

    She _____ _____ with the history of the company.

11. **insist on** sthg. = to accept only certain things, to require

    They _____ _____ exercising before school.

    They _____ _____ doing it.

12. **major in** sthg. = to pursue academic studies in a major

    Larry _____ _____ computer science.

    Sergey _____ _____ it, too.

13. **show up** = to arrive; to appear

    The students _____ _____ to class on time.

    I clicked a link, and a graphic image _____ _____

    on the screen.

ACTIVITY 22   **Using phrasal verbs in dialogues**

Complete the following dialogues. Use the words in parentheses. Use the past tense of the phrasal verbs given in the question. Use pronouns. The first two answers are done for you.

Practice the dialogues with a partner. Speak with good stress, intonation, and linking.

1. A: Where did she look up the answers to the test? (on the teacher's webpage)

    B: *She looked them up on the teacher's webpage.*

2. A: Where did you fill up your car? (at the gas station across from the college)

    B: *I filled it up at the gas station across from the college.*

3. A: Did he make out the check to you? (No, my company)

    B: _____

4. A: When did they set up their business? (about five years ago)

    B: _____

5. A: Did you hook up your computer to the Internet? (Yes, last month)

    B: _____

6. A: How did you think up that great idea? (in a dream last week)

    B: _____

7. A: Did your sister go into law or medicine? (medicine)

    B: _____

8. A: What did your brother major in? (history)

    B: _____

9. A: What time did the guests show up at the party? (around 8 o'clock)

    B: _____

10. (Write your own dialogue with a phrasal verb.)

    A: _____

    B: _____

ACTIVITY 23 Using rising intonation on tag questions

As you learned in Chapter 5, a tag question is added to a statement when the speaker wants confirmation or agreement from the listener. If an American speaker is not sure that the statement is true, the tag is spoken with rising intonation. The speaker is asking for confirmation: "I want to make sure" or "I hope so." Compare the following sentences from the lecture:

That was an **easy** one, **wasn't** it? (falling)	The instructor believes the test item was easy.
You've heard of Google, **haven't** you? (rising)	The instructor supposes the students have probably heard of Google but is not sure.

Listen to the following sentences with rising tag questions. Underline the stressed words where the intonation changes in the statement and in the tag. Mark the rising and falling intonation with arrows, The first one is done for you.

You all got your <u>tests</u> back, <u>didn't</u> you? (rising)

This value is the only reason you go to the gas station, isn't it? (rising)

They didn't want to just throw it[3] into a drawer, did they? (rising)

You can look them[4] up, can't you? (rising)

Underline the word that should be stressed in the statement and in the tag. Mark the rising and falling intonation with arrows. The first one is done for you. Then practice pronouncing the sentences until you can say them smoothly.

1. You know where the professor's <u>office</u> is, <u>don't</u> you? (I hope you can tell me where it is.)

2. You don't have an extra twenty dollars, do you? (I need $20. You probably don't have it, but I'll ask anyway.)

3. You weren't absent on the test day, were you? (I don't think you were absent, but I'm not sure.)

4. You took the test, didn't you? (I hope you took the test. Then we can discuss it.)

5. There's no test today, is there? (I hope there's no test today.)

6. You aren't majoring in business, are you?

7. You weren't born in this state, were you?

8. You can speak two languages, can't you?

9. You've heard of Yahoo, haven't you?

10. The teacher gave us an assignment, didn't she/he?

3. *it* = the check for a hundred thousand dollars
4. *them* = the number of searches Google handles and the number of webpages it gives users access to

ACTIVITY 24 **Answering tag questions and adding details**

When we answer a question with *Yes* or *No*, we often add details.

With your class, discuss the differences between the following pairs of dialogues. Which dialogues are friendlier? Why?

Example 1a:

| Tag question: | A: | You know where the professor's office is, don't you? |
| Short answer: | B: | Yes, I do. |

Example 1b:

Tag question:	A:	You know where the professor's office is, don't you?
Answer + detail:	B:	Yes, I do. It's L320, on the third floor of Building L.
Response:	A:	Thanks a lot. I'll go there during office hours.

Example 2a:

| Tag question: | A: | You know where the professor's office is, don't you? |
| Short answer: | B: | No, I don't. |

Example 2b:

Tag question:	A:	You know where the professor's office is, don't you?
Answer + detail:	B:	No, I'm sorry, I don't. Maybe Sal knows.
Response:	A:	Okay. Thanks, anyway. I'll ask Sal.

With a partner, create a dialogue for each tag question, like the ones above. Add details. When you answer a tag question, use No *with a negative verb. Use* Yes *with an affirmative verb.*

1. **A:** You know where our professor's <u>office</u> is, <u>don't</u> you?

    B: _____

    A: _____

2. **A:** You don't have an extra twenty dollars, do you?

    B: _____

    A: _____

3. **A:** You weren't absent on the test day, were you?

   B: _____

   A: _____

4. **A:** You took the test, didn't you?

   B: _____

   A: _____

5. **A:** There's no test today, is there?

   B: _____

   A: _____

6. **A:** You aren't majoring in business, are you?

   B: _____

   A: _____

7. **A:** You weren't born in this state, were you?

   B: _____

   A: _____

8. **A:** You can speak two languages, can't you?

   B: _____

   A: _____

9. **A:** You've heard of Yahoo, haven't you?

   B: _____

   A: _____

10. **A:** The teacher gave us an assignment, didn't she/he?

    B: _____

    A: _____

11. **A:** (Your own tag question)

    B: _____

    A: _____

Practice the dialogues you created. Take turns. When you ask the question, use rising intonation on the tag.

POWER GRAMMAR

Time Phrases with Prepositions

We use different prepositions to talk about time:

<u>on</u> Monday, <u>on</u> Thursday	on + a day of the week
<u>in</u> the morning, <u>in</u> the afternoon, <u>in</u> the evening	in + a part of a day
<u>before</u> noon, <u>after</u> class	before/after + time/activity
<u>at</u> five o'clock, <u>at</u> two-thirty	at + a specific clock time
<u>from</u> ten o'clock <u>to</u> ten thirty	from + beginning… to + end

ACTIVITY 25 **Talking about Jessica's agenda**

*Look at Jessica's agenda from last week. Answer the questions. Use the correct form of the past tense. Use the correct prepositions. Afterward, check the **Answer Box** on the next page.*

1. When did Jessica attend her geography class?

   _____

2. Did Jessica wait tables at Max's Coffee Shop from 1:00 to 2:30 on Sunday?

   _____

3. Jessica conducted experiments in her biology lab on Friday afternoon, didn't she?

   _____

4. Jessica didn't play tennis with Allison on Wednesday, did she?

   _____

5. Did Jessica have lunch with Hugo before or after her geography class?

   _____

6. (Ask and answer your own question about Jessica's biology class.)

   _____

   _____

Jessica's agenda (last week)							
	Sunday	**Monday**	**Tuesday**	**Wednesday**	**Thursday**	**Friday**	**Saturday**
8:00		geography class		geography class		geography class	
8:30							
9:00					conduct experiments in biology lab		
9:30							
10:00		study at library	biology class				
10:30	play tennis with Allison						
11:00							wait tables at Max's Coffee Shop
11:30				have lunch with Hugo			
12:00							
12:30							
1:00							
1:30							

Answer Box

1. She attended her geography class on Monday, Wednesday and Friday at 8:00.
2. No, she didn't. She waited tables at Max's Coffee Shop from 11:00 to 2:00 on Saturday.
3. No, she didn't. She conducted experiments in her biology lab on Thursday morning (from 9:00 to 12:00).
4. No, she didn't. She played tennis with Allison on Sunday (at 10:30/from 10:30 to 12:00).
5. She had lunch with Hugo after her geography class on Wednesday (at 11:30/from 11:30 to 1:00.)
6. Possible questions: When did Jessica attend her biology class? Jessica attended her biology class on Thursday afternoon, didn't she? Jessica didn't attend her biology class at 1:00 on Friday, did she? Did Jessica attend her biology class from 12:00 to 1:30 on Tuesday?

ACTIVITY 26   Filling in an agenda

In this activity, you will practice giving and receiving information about a student's agenda from last week. You will ask and answer questions in the past tense. You will use time phrases. Use the previous activity as a model.

Work in pairs. Decide who is Partner A and who is Partner B.

Partner A	Partner B
▪ *Look at page 252.* ▪ *You have a blank agenda for Bob. Ask the questions on the next page about Bob's week.* ▪ *Listen to your partner's information. Fill in Bob's agenda on your page.* ▪ *You have Allison's agenda from last week. Answer your partner's question about Allison's week.* ▪ *Do NOT look at your partner's page until both of you finish the activity.*	▪ *Look at page 264.* ▪ *You have Bob's agenda from last week. Answer your partner's question about Bob's week.* ▪ *When it is your turn, ask the questions on your page about Allison's week. You have a blank agenda for Allison.* ▪ *Listen to your partner's information. Fill in Allison's agenda on your page.* ▪ *Do NOT look at your partner's page until both of you finish the activity.*

ACTIVITY 27   Learning to search the Web

Accessing the World Wide Web

To find information on the Web, you need to use a computer with Internet access. The computer must have a Web browser such as Microsoft Internet Explorer or Netscape Communicator. You may find a computer with Internet access at a college library, a public library, a computer lab, a workplace, an Internet café, and/or your own home.

In the Web address box, type http:// followed by the Web address of the search engine, for example http://www.google.com. Once you are at the search engine website, you may begin your search for information on your topic.

Read below to learn some tips on how to begin your search. Refer to the figures on the opposite page.

- DO use the most common words that describe your search.

- DON'T be afraid to type in keywords that come to mind.

Google quickly returns results and makes it easy to search and find new words and phrases. For example, try searching for the author of this textbook, the name of your college, or the name of your hobby (e.g., *stamp collecting* or *Chinese cooking*).

- DO what seems obvious[5] first.

- DON'T be afraid. Type in single or multiple keywords.

Search for Keywords

- DON'T write a question or sentence.
  For example, if you want to see Internet pages about Charlie Chaplin, don't type Who was Charlie Chaplin? or I want to know about Charlie Chaplin.
  Type in Charlie Chaplin.

5. **obvious** (*adj.*) Easy to see or understand, clear.

- DO use correct spelling.
  For example, if you are looking for information about Bill Cosby, the American comedian, be sure to type Bill Cosby and not Bill Cosbey.

- DONT worry about case. bill Cosby, Bill Cosby and BILL COSBY give the same results.

- DO provide several keywords to narrow the search.
  Suppose you want information about Robin Williams, the American comedian, in his role as Mrs. Doubtfire. If you enter Robin Williams, you get at least 1,250,000 results.
  If you enter Robin Williams comedian, the results decrease to 26,000.
  If you enter Robin Williams American comedian, the results decrease to 11,700.
  If you enter Robin Williams American comedian Mrs Doubtfire, the results decrease to 405.

Try Using Quotes

- DO use quotation marks if you want to perform a *phrase search*.
  For example, if you enter "robin williams" "american comedian" "mrs doubtfire", the search engine will search for pages that have three two-word phrases and not six single words. You may get only nine results. You decide if it's helpful or not.

Read the Summary Text

- DO read the phrases from the webpages. This summary text will give you an idea of the content of the webpage.

- DO choose the best results from there.

Figure 1

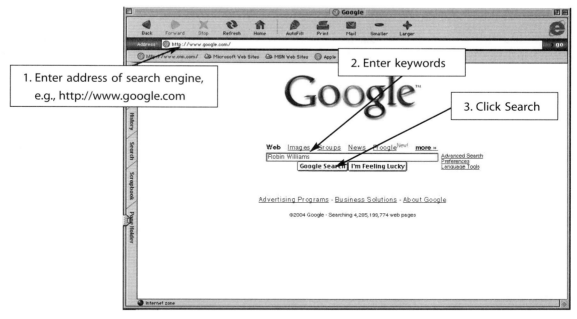

Opening search page: Robin Williams

Figure 2

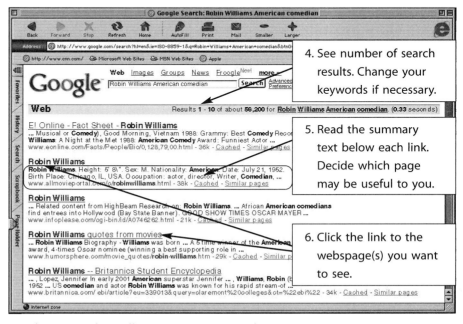

Results page: robin williams american comedian

With a partner, ask and answer these questions;

1. What do you need to search the Web? (Underline and state all that apply.)
   a. a computer
   b. a connection to the Internet
   c. an email address
   d. a Web browser
   e. a library card

2. You type the Web address of the search engine into the address box, don't you?

   _____

   _____

3. If you use Google as your search engine, exactly what do you type to get to that website?

   _____

   _____

4. Which word or words should you type in the search box?

   _____

   _____

5. Do you need to type a complete sentence with good spelling, capitalization, and punctuation? Explain.

   _____

   _____

6. Which gives you more results: one word or many words? Is one better than the other?

   _____

   _____

7. Are you ready to search the Web for information?

   _____

   _____

ACTIVITY 28 Preparing a report about a business

Some businesses have an interesting history, and you can find out about them on the Web, and in books, magazines, and newspapers.

With your class, discuss the businesses below.[6] *Add others to the list.*

Papa John's

John started this pizza business as a high school student. He thought that "there was something missing from national pizza chains: a superior-quality traditional pizza delivered to the customer's door."

Burt's Bees

This company sells "earth friendly natural personal care products." According to their website, Burt started his company as a beekeeper. His company bottled honey and sold beeswax polish. Gradually they added more products to their line.

eBay

Pierre Omidyar knew that people needed a central location to buy and sell unusual items. Buyers and sellers with similar interests needed a location to meet. He started this online trading company to meet these needs.

Celestial Seasonings

This tea company began in Colorado. Mo and Peggy Siegel gathered wild herbs in the Rocky Mountains. With partners, they made them into healthful teas. They created more teas and dietary supplements.

The Body Shop

This company is a "values driven, high quality skin and body care retailer." Founder Anita Roddick started in England. She insisted on protecting animals and the environment for her products by using natural ingredients.

6. Log into the course website for details on how to get more information on these companies.

Dave's ESL Café

Founder Dave Sperling bought a Macintosh computer, realized the power of the Internet for communication, and started "The Internet's Meeting Place for ESL/EFL Students and Teachers from Around the World."

Tiger Balm

Chinese herbalists and healers used this soothing herbal balm for their patients. Aw Boon Haw used creative marketing methods to build a fortune around Tiger Balm.

Others:

_____

_____

_____

_____

_____

_____

_____

_____

_____

_____

Choose a business that you are interested in. Use library books, magazines, and Web resources to find information about it. Take notes about its history. Some questions to consider are as follows:

- What product(s) does the business have? Are they goods, services, or both? Does the business sell them or offer them free?
- Who uses the company's product(s)? Describe this company's customers.
- Who is/are the entrepreneur(s) of this business? What is their background?
- How did the entrepreneur(s) start? How did the business develop?
- In what way did this business create value for its customers? What does it provide that the customer is willing to pay for?

ACTIVITY 29   **Presenting information about a business**

Case study: In a group of four students, tell your partners about the business you researched. Your instructor will let you know if you may use your written report as a guide. Use past tense about the history and present tense about present conditions. Try to use one tag question and one transition as in Chapter 5. When you are listening to a partner's presentation, repeat key information for confirmation and clarification. Ask about meaning and differences. Take brief notes in the chart below.

Partner's name			
Business			
Entrepreneur(s)			
Product(s)			
History			
Value for customers			
Other interesting points			

Activity 26 Partner A Partner B, turn to page 264

1. You have a blank agenda for Bob. Ask the questions on the next page about Bob's week. Listen to your partner's information. Fill in Bob's agenda. Do NOT look at your partner's page.

2. You have Allison's agenda. Your partner has a blank agenda for Allison. Listen to your partner's questions about Allison's week. Give your partner information from Allison's agenda. Use the correct form of the past tense in your answers. Use the correct prepositions.

3. After you and your partner finish asking and answering, check each other's agendas.

Bob's agenda (last week)							
	Sunday	**Monday**	**Tuesday**	**Wednesday**	**Thursday**	**Friday**	**Saturday**
8:00							
8:30							
9:00							
9:30							
10:00							
10:30							
11:00							
11:30							
12:00							
12:30							
1:00							
1:30							

Questions

1. When did Bob visit the professor?
2. Did Bob go to his algebra class at 10 o'clock on Tuesday?
3. Bob studied for chemistry from 9:30 to 11:30 on Friday, didn't he?
4. Bob didn't play basketball on Thursday, did he?
5. Did Bob work on his project in the computer lab before or after his English class?
6. What did Bob do on Friday?
7. (Ask your own question about Bob's psychology class.)

Allison's Agenda (last week)							
	Sunday	**Monday**	**Tuesday**	**Wednesday**	**Thursday**	**Friday**	**Saturday**
2:00		Nutrition class				Music appreciation class	
2:30				Research a company's history for case study			
3:00					Write paper for American literature class		
3:30			Conduct Physics lab experiment				
4:00							
4:30	Serve dinner at the homeless shelter						Babysit neighbor's children
5:00							
5:30							
6:00							
6:30		Attend soccer practice		Attend soccer practice			
7:00							
7:30							

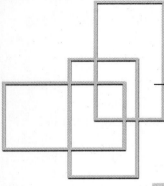

Part 3

ASSESSING YOUR LISTENING AND SPEAKING SKILLS

ACTIVITY 30 Applying information and skills

Your instructor may ask you to write down the answers to the questions, discuss these questions in a group, and/or record your oral answers to the questions.

1. What is the meaning of each of the following business terms? Use it in a sentence that shows the meaning.

    a. product _____

    b. service _____

    c. customer _____

    d. purchase _____

    e. create value _____

    f. profit _____

    g. loss _____

    h. entrepreneur _____

2. How can a case study help you learn the concepts of a course?

    _____

    _____

    _____

3. What did you learn about searching the web for information?

    _____

    _____

    _____

4. How has your understanding and use of computer technology changed in the last two or three years?

   _____

   _____

   _____

5. When should you use /t/, /d/ and /ɪd/ verb endings? Explain your answer, and give two examples of each.

   _____

   _____

   _____

   _____

6. If you are talking about time, when should you use the prepositions below? Explain your answer, and give two examples of each.

   a. at   _____

   b. on   _____

   c. in   _____

   d. before _____

   e. after   _____

   f. from . . . to _____

7. What is the difference between saying a tag question with falling intonation and saying a tag question with rising intonation? Compare the two sentences and explain the difference in meaning.

   Sentence 1   Sentence 2

   The author's last name is Chan,   She's from California,

   isn't it?   isn't she?

   _____

   _____

   _____

ACTIVITY 31 Pronunciation, stress and fluency

Review these words and dialogues. Write the syllable-stress code for words 1–12. Draw intonation lines over the keywords in dialogues 13–16. Then practice with a partner. Pronounce each item as clearly and fluently as you can. Have your partner listen and help you with your pronunciation of syllables, stress and intonation. Take turns. Your instructor may ask you to record your pronunciation of these items and others in this chapter.

1. invest [___ - ___]   7. relevant [___ - ___]

2. profit [___ - ___]   8. secure [___ - ___]

3. business [___ - ___]   9. establish [___ - ___]

4. available [___ - ___]   10. income [___ - ___]

5. credit [___ - ___]   11. purchase [___ - ___]

6. Internet [___ - ___]   12. technology [___ - ___]

13. **A:** Did you look up the word in the dictionary?

   B: Yes, I looked it up in an online dictionary.

14. **A:** He majored in computer science, didn't he?

   B: No, he majored in mathematics.

15. **A:** The professor posted her office hours, didn't she?

   B: Yes, she posted them on the wall outside her door.

16. **A:** I handed in the right assignment, didn't I?

   B: Yes, you handed in the right one.

ACTIVITY 32 Hearing syllables and word stress

Listen carefully to ten words from the chapter. You will hear each word once. Listen for the number of syllables and the stressed syllable. Write the syllable-stress code in the brackets.

1. [___ - ___]   5. [___ - ___]   8. [___ - ___]

2. [___ - ___]   6. [___ - ___]   9. [___ - ___]

3. [___ - ___]   7. [___ - ___]   10. [___ - ___]

4. [___ - ___]

ACTIVITY 33 Taking dictation

In this dictation you will hear vocabulary and sentence patterns that you practiced in this chapter. Your instructor will tell you the number of words in each sentence. Write the numbers within the parentheses and use them as a guide. You will hear each sentence three times. First, listen and try to understand the meaning of the whole sentence. Second, listen and write. Third, listen and check.

1. _____ (_____words)

   _____ (_____words)

2. _____ (_____words)

   _____ (_____words)

3. _____ (_____words)

   _____ (_____words)

4. _____ (_____words)

   _____ (_____words)

5. _____ (_____words)

   _____ (_____words)

6. _____ (_____words)

   _____ (_____words)

7. _____ (_____words)

   _____ (_____words)

8. _____ (_____words)

   _____ (_____words)

ACTIVITY 34 Summarizing your progress

How well can you perform the following objectives?

I can . . .	Barely	Somewhat	Fairly well	Very well
Use vocabulary and expressions to discuss business and technology.				
Use a dictionary to learn the pronunciation of new academic words.				
Pronounce key vocabulary with proper syllables and word stress.				
Pronounce past tense verbs with -ed endings: /t/, /d/ and /ɪd/				
Tell how a case study can deepen understanding of concepts.				
Understand and use new phrasal verbs.				
Understand and use tag questions with rising intonation.				
Ask and answer questions using regular and irregular past tense forms.				
Relate the contents of the lecture to my use of technology.				
Take dictation of sentences related to business and technology.				

WEB POWER

You will find additional exercises related to the content in this chapter at http://esl.college.hmco.com/students.

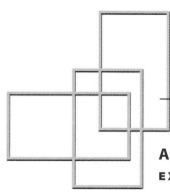

Appendices

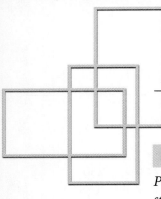

Appendix 1

ACTIVITY 24 Exchanging and confirming information

Partner B, this appendix is for you. Partner A look at page 64. Take turns speaking, listening, and confirming information about nutrition and health.

Partner A: Read sentence 1. Partner B: Listen, ask one or more questions for clarification or confirmation.

Partner A: Respond to Partner B's questions. Partner B: Take notes.

Partner B: Read sentence 1. Partner A: Listen, ask one or more questions for clarification or confirmation.

Partner B: Respond to Partner A's questions. Partner A: Take notes.

Partner A: Read sentence 2, and so on.

Partner B: Read sentence 2, and so on.

Continue taking turns in this way until you finish or until your instructor tells you to stop.

Confirm	My partner's number phrases
1. ☐	_____
2. ☐	_____
3. ☐	_____
4. ☐	_____
5. ☐	_____
6. ☐	_____

Partner B: Read one sentence at a time to Partner A. Use the words in parentheses to help you pronounce the numbers.

1. Most babies start to grow teeth between six and ten months of age.
2. There are two grams of fiber in two tablespoons of peanut butter.
3. A cup of spaghetti with meat sauce contains about 332 (three hundred thirty-two) calories.
4. A typical person should consume less than 30 (thirty) percent of calories from fat.
5. Every day, we should eat 3–5 (three to five) servings from the vegetable group and 2–4 (two to four) servings from the fruit group.
6. Here are some typical servings of protein-rich foods: 2–3 (two to three) ounces of lean cooked meat, poultry, or fish; one egg; and 1/2 (a half) cup of cooked dried beans.

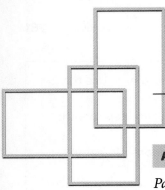

Appendix 2

CHAPTER 3

ACTIVITY 26 Placing the cities on the map

Partner B, this appendix is for you. Partner A look at page 112. You and your partner have different information. You will exchange information orally. When it is your turn to read a sentence, pronounce clearly with the correct number of syllables and with good stress. When it is your turn to listen, check and confirm your understanding. Ask questions such as Excuse me. What is the latitude? Please repeat the longitude. Did you say ___? How do you spell ___? *Fill in the name of the city on your map. Take turns speaking and listening. Do not look at each other's maps yet!*

1. Montgomery is located at 32 degrees north latitude and 86 degrees west longitude.
2. Washington, D.C., is located at 39 degrees north latitude and 77 degrees west longitude.
3. San Francisco is located at 38 degrees north latitude and 122 degrees west longitude.
4. Cincinnati is located at 39 degrees north latitude and 84 degrees west longitude.
5. At 48 degrees north latitude and 88 degrees west longitude, you will find Chicago.
6. At 40 degrees north latitude and 75 degrees west longitude, you will find Philadelphia.

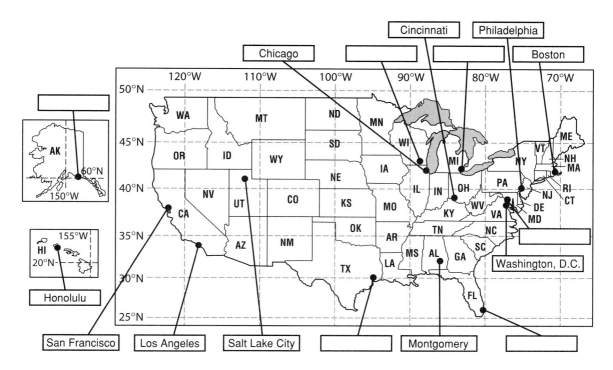

*After filling in all the missing cities, check your map with your partner.
Then continue with Activity 27 on pages 111–112.*

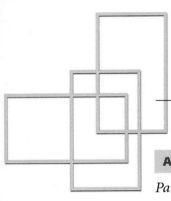

Appendix 3

CHAPTER 6

ACTIVITY 26 Filling in an agenda

Partner B, this appendix if for you. Partner A look at page 252.

1. *You have Bob's agenda. Your partner has a blank agenda for Bob. Listen to your partner's questions about Bob's week. Give your partner information from Bob's agenda. Use the correct form of the past tense in your answers. Use the correct prepositions.*

2. *You have a blank agenda for Allison. Ask the questions on your page about Allison's week. Listen to your partner's information. Fill in Allison's agenda. Do NOT look at your partner's page.*

3. *After you and your partner finish asking and answering, check each other's agendas.*

Bob's agenda (last week)							
	Sunday	**Monday**	**Tuesday**	**Wednesday**	**Thursday**	**Friday**	**Saturday**
8:00							
8:30		Visit Prof. Ross L320	English class		Psychology class		
9:00	Play basketball						
9:30						Paint picture for art class	
10:00				Algebra class			
10:30							
11:00							
11:30			Work on project in computer lab				Study for chemistry
12:00							
12:30							
1:00							
1:30							

Questions

1. When did Allison research a company's history for a case study?
2. Allison attended soccer practice at 6:30 on Tuesday and Thursday, didn't she?
3. Did Allison go to nutrition class before or after soccer practice?
4. Allison didn't baby-sit her neighbor's children on Sunday afternoon, did she?
5. Allison served dinner at the homeless shelter from 4:30 to 7:00 on Friday, didn't she?
7. (Ask your own question about Allison's music appreciation class.)

_____

_____

_____

Allison's agenda (last week)							
	Sunday	Monday	Tuesday	Wednesday	Thursday	Friday	Saturday
2:00							
2:30							
3:00							
3:30							
4:00							
4:30							
5:00							
5:30							
6:00							
6:30							
7:00							
7:30							